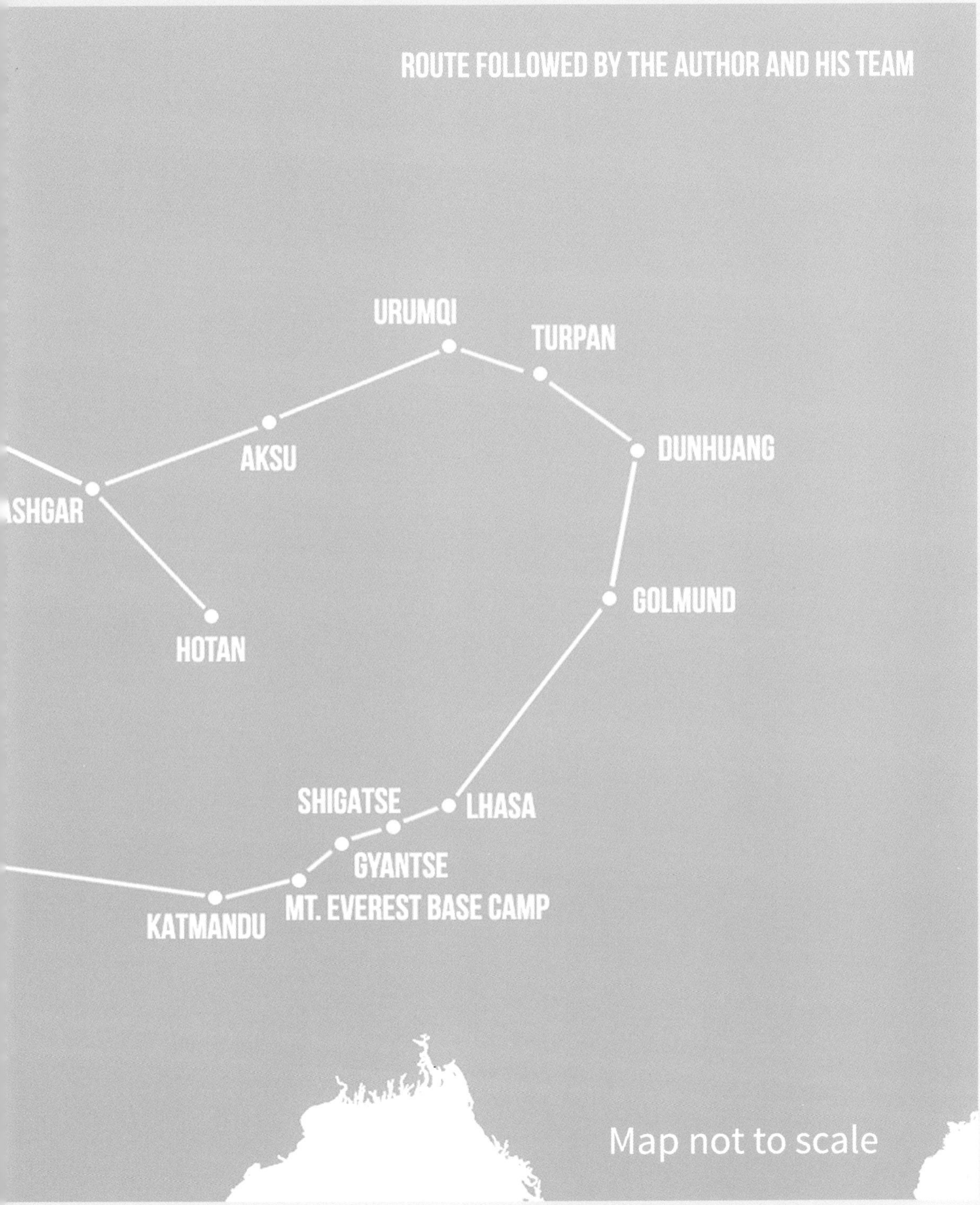

ROUTE FOLLOWED BY THE AUTHOR AND HIS TEAM
URUMQI
TURPAN
AKSU
DUNHUANG
ASHGAR
GOLMUND
HOTAN
SHIGATSE
LHASA
GYANTSE
MT. EVEREST BASE CAMP
KATMANDU
Map not to scale

BEYOND THE HIMALAYAS

BEYOND THE HIMALAYAS

JOURNEYING THROUGH THE SILK ROUTE

Text: GOUTAM GHOSE & MICHAEL HAGGIAG

Photographs: GOUTAM GHOSE

Foreword: KUNAL BASU

NIYOGI
BOOKS

Published by
NIYOGI BOOKS
Block D, Building No. 77
Okhla Industrial Area, Phase-I
New Delhi-110 020, INDIA
Tel: 91-11-26816301, 26818960
Email: niyogibooks@gmail.com
Website: www.niyogibooksindia.com

Cover photographs: Goutam Ghose

Editor: Sucharita Ghosh
Design: Pinaki De

ISBN: 978-93-86906-89-2
Publication: 2019

Printed at: Niyogi Offset Pvt. Ltd., New Delhi, India

To Major H.P.S. Ahluwalia

店
商店

CONTENTS

FOREWORD

There is no place more enchanting than this. The collective trove of memories alone entices scholars and artistic pretenders from the world over. Civilizations have emerged from these varied terrains steeped in the lore of love and war. A land known as much for many fabled journeys as it is for its ancient and modern travellers. You could say it is the original melting pot. It is the Silk Road. And like all roads it has a beginning and an end. Or does it?

'Life is a spiritual journey,' Goutam Ghose writes, 'whose final aim is liberation from worldly worries.' The landmarks of one's journey might be the mountains one climbs, the deserts crossed in extreme heat and cold; or much admired pastures that tempt a nomadic soul. No matter how long it lasts, it gives much and takes much, rarely leaving any stones unturned. And the same goes for chronicles of enchanting journeys, like those undertaken by Ghose and his friends over countless miles and countless days.

Beyond the Himalayas isn't the first of a traveller's account, but unique for the author's voracious appetite savouring every bit of the landscape. The mind's eye shows more than what his lens captures: a once borderless world of nomads, travelling monks, empire builders and mystics. Timur and Ghenghis rub shoulders with Mullah Nasiruddin and Baha-ud-Din Naqshband. The shadow of Xuanzang, the seventh-century Buddhist pilgrim, can be seen fleeting across sand dunes. Cocking one's ears one hears the neighing warhorses of Babur, the first Mughal emperor, grazing the grasslands of his native Fergana. Then there are the early European explorers – Aurel Stein, Sven Hedin, Albert von Le Coq – and their grand expeditions, revered and reviled for digging up the stories of Central Asia from their remains under the inhospitable earth.

Wisely, Goutam Ghose's photo-chronicle has sought to build rich narrative veins around the many-splendored cities treating them as landmarks across times and civilizations: Samarkand

and Bukhara fabled as much for the past glories of Timur's clan as they are for manifesting the soul of the fledgling Uzbek republic. Babur's Fergana, once doomed to history's backwaters, revived by the great Soviet canal project with thousands of toiling workers rivalling the feats of the Mughal horsemen digging up a 270 km stretch to flood the wasteland. It's Ghose's cinematic mind that transposes images across centuries, conjuring up more than the cities themselves to bring home a continuing tapestry of human existence. There are no side characters in this grand epic, and the author delights with his sketches – the delectable cameo performances – all through his route: the storyteller of Khotan, the tea drinkers of Bukhara, Rawat – descendant of Kishen Singh who the British had sent into Tibet as a spy disguised as a Buddhist pilgrim, bored soldiers at checkpoints, and cackling children that meet the travellers at every bend of the road.

And then, there are the towering characters: Major Hari Ahluwalia, the much decorated and disabled army man, the guiding spirit behind this journey who'd sought to build a bridge between India and China the only way possible: by crossing the mountain in between. Michael, the Western Buddhist, making his own private journey following the trail of an ancient Chinese pilgrim who'd travelled to India in search of the Buddha.

Mythical caravan stops abound as Ghose travels eastward: Bishkek, the capital of Kyrgyzstan, Kashgar – known by the local Uighur as Kashi – oasis towns on the Taklamakan like Yarkand, Khotan, Urumqi and Dunhuang with its cave of a thousand Buddhas. And then Tibet. Like every explorer, the reader too holds his/her breath as the travelling party encounters 'the most stupendous upheaval to be found on the face of the planet.' It is also the time for dizziness, headache, nausea, and a strange heaviness of the chest. Here too, as elsewhere, Ghose treats the reader to a cinematic jump-cut to narrate separate journeys undertaken by early women travellers to Tibet: Ann Taylor, Susie Reinhardt, and Alexandra David-Néel, the first European woman to become a Tibetan Lama. By now the stage is set for mountain yaks, Lhasa and the Potala.

Beyond the Himalayas is more than travel anecdotes. More than retelling of history. Even more than a stream of startling pictures of a less travelled land. In the end its reach is more than the destinations that it covers. 'Shatter the goblet, fall for the glassblower's breath' – Rumi the mystic lover-poet had so written. The breath reveals the real story, not the goblet that it forms for eyes to admire. It is the breath of the filmmaker, traveller, romantic – ever inquisitive, ever in wonder – that is bound to leave the reader breathless when the last page has been turned.

Kunal Basu
Oxford

INTRODUCTION

Alexander Pushkin wrote, 'Everything is a sacrifice to your memory.' I would add 'a sacrifice to a garland of memories' that pulsate throughout one's life and beyond. The so-called 'present' is a fraction of fractions between the past and the future and hence the present moments are stored in our memory as recent or remote past. We live with memories as long as our mind functions and then we remain in the memory of others surviving in a linear frame of time. This book narrates one such vivid memory, a once-in-a-lifetime kind of adventure.

A few years back I opened a cupboard full of old negatives, slides and some faded prints. I was shocked to see hundreds of neatly stacked slides were covered with fungus. As I started going through them, all I saw was our caravan of Mahindra Armada jeeps plying through the meandering valleys and endless deserts of the fabled Silk Road. I was fortunate enough to be a part of the Central Asian expedition organized by Major H.P.S. Ahluwalia way back in 1994. My film *Beyond the Himalayas* was the result of our fourteen-thousand-kilometre journey through Central Asia, China and Tibet. The film was produced by British producer Michael Haggiag, Doordarshan (India) and Youth Exploration Society. The five-part series was shown extensively by Discovery, Doordarshan and BBC in the late 1990s. But, unfortunately, the film was forgotten in later years, barring a few scattered screenings. Respected professor of history Barun De had used the series as a part of his lectures on Central Asia in Maulana Azad Institute of Central Asian Studies and later advised me to write a book on this incredible journey. Then the real driving force came from the late Suresh Neotia, eminent chairman emeritus of the Ambuja Group and a philanthropist, who told me after watching the series, 'Why don't you make a film-book which may remain for posterity!'

As far as the text is concerned, a large section has been taken from the narration of the original soundtrack of the series. And some chapters were freshly written for the book.

I humbly present you this bouquet of memories.

Goutam Ghose
Kolkata

The author with the people of Fergana

THE OTHER SIDE OF THE MOUNTAIN

Major Hari Ahluwalia was a young officer in the Indian Army when he climbed Everest in 1965. He was a member of the first Indian expedition to successfully scale the mountain and one of the first to reach the summit. Our then prime minister, Jawaharlal Nehru, awarded him India's coveted Arjuna Award and India had a new national hero. But within two months of receiving the award, he was wounded in combat along the India-Pakistan border and permanently disabled. Despite the setback, Hari continued organizing mountaineering expeditions and writing books about his life and travels.

It was as the chairman of the Youth Exploring Society of India that he invited me to film an expedition he was planning along an ancient trade route connecting India with Central Asia and Tibet. But most of the route lay within modern China. This would be the first time any group was being allowed to make a journey with its own vehicles – a diplomatic breakthrough and a personal triumph for Hari.

Hari and the Chinese Delegation

In 1962, a border dispute between India and China had erupted into a brief war which left the two countries estranged for the next thirty years. In the two most populous nations of the world, a generation of young people had grown up, knowing little or nothing about one another.

Hari's idea was to encourage peaceful dialogue between India and her northern neighbour through new cultural exchanges. In Beijing, he met with the president of the Disabled Federation, who, like Hari, is confined to a wheelchair. As it happened, he is also the son of China's leader, Chairman Deng Xiaoping, and is thus perfectly placed to help Hari fulfil his dream.

I live in Calcutta and I make films about India. My country was run by the British for 200 years, yet it preserves an ancient culture that conditions every aspect of its daily life. Because we live in a world of our own, separated from the north by politics and geography, I have always wanted to see what lay just a few hundred miles from me on the other side of the mountains. Excited about Hari's proposal, I abandoned my new idea for a feature film and began to think about journeying along the ancient Silk Road.

The first place I decided to visit was The Asiatic Society. Founded by Sir William Jones in 1784, the society pioneered the rediscovery of Asia and its past. All the early expeditions were organized and monitored from here. I was suddenly filled with curiosity and an impetuous desire to delve into all the rare books and manuscripts on its shelves. *The Travels of Marco Polo* describe the wonders of the Silk Road – cities far greater than his own and a world more magnificent than anything imagined by the insular backward Europe of the thirteenth century. But he was a late traveller. The Silk Route was one of the greatest trade routes in history and men had already been travelling there for four thousand years. Before sea routes were discovered in the fifteenth century, this trans-Asian highway was the sole link between the east and the west. It ran from Xi'an in China all the way to the Mediterranean. There were, moreover, many tributaries to the mighty river, not least of which were caravan routes across the Himalayan mountain range between India and Central Asia.

A facsimile of Hari's letter to me –

Dear Goutam,
You will be delighted to know that we now have all our permissions. Because of the current turmoil in Afghanistan, we cannot drive through the Khyber Pass into the Central Asia as planned. All the members of the expedition including the jeeps and equipment will be flown from Delhi to Uzbekistan on the 18th of May.
I believe I told you about my London-based friend Michael, who is a filmmaker with a longstanding interest in Buddhism. He has wanted to make this trip for a long time and I'm sure he will be immensely helpful to you. Do please get in touch with him.

The author with Michael Haggiag and his wife Katherine in front of their house at London

As per Hari's suggestion I met Michael Haggiag in his London home. Michael was preparing for the trip with great excitement. I filmed him and his wife there.

A conversation between Michael and his wife Katherine in London –

Katherine – 'Want some tea?'

Michael thanks her. 'This is what Marco Polo had to say about the women of Hami and their very nice customs.

I give you my word – when a stranger comes to a house here to seek hospitality, he receives a very warm welcome.

The host makes his wife do everything the guest wishes and he leaves the house and goes about his own business and stays away for two or three days. Meanwhile, the guest stays with his wife in the house and does what he will with her – lying with her in one bed, just as if she was his own wife, and they lead a gay life together. The women are beautiful and vivacious and always ready to oblige.

'I am not sending you there.'

'No? It's also very hot. It's 40°C in the shade – that's over 100°F. They also have the largest cockroaches.'

'Sounds like it's terrible out there!'

'Anyway, I'm preparing for the trip. Look at these wonderful books here … this is Bukhara and this, Samarkand … these are some really old pictures of the way it was in the 1890s!'

'Beautiful places!'

'Do you realize how long Hari had to wait for permission for this? He started organizing his expedition eight years ago and he just got confirmation now. And if we don't go within the next three weeks, we can't go at all.'

~

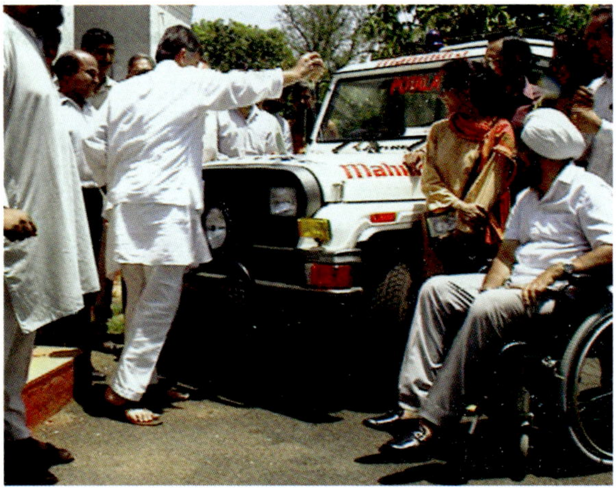

Madhav Rao Scindia wishing good luck

On the day of our departure, we all assembled at Hari's home in Delhi and waited for our jeeps to arrive. The expedition includes Central Asian scholars, scientists, doctors as well as professional rally drivers and mechanics. At this moment, however, we seem more like a group of excited tourists. As we are about to set off, a coconut is broken open on one of our jeeps – the traditional Indian way of wishing good luck.

Our flight over the Himalayas is brief but spectacular. At last, we are appearing beyond the great mountain range that divides India from the rest of Asia. I find it hard to imagine how the old camel caravans could have travelled through such a forbidding landscape! What impact could our divided worlds have had upon one another, separated as they were by such an enormous barrier!

Look 'round thee now on Samarkand!
Is she not Queen of Earth? Her pride
Above all cities? In her hand
Their destinies? In all beside
Of glory which the world hath known
Stands she not nobly and alone?

– 'Tamerlane' by Edgar Allan Poe

The Armada starts its journey

Guri Amir mausoleum, Samarkand

Our first port of call is the ancient city of Samarkand. In the fourteenth century, it became the legendary capital of Timur the Lame or Tamerlane, who subjugated the whole of Central Asia with his scorched earth policy but made Samarkand grander and more beautiful than any city before it. Within the mosque complex of Bibi-Khanym lies the Guri Amir mausoleum where Timur and his descendants are all buried.

Samarkand was liberal and free-thinking under Timur and his successors. There was no gender bias in education and scientific research flourished. The tympanums of the main portal of the Madrasah or high school represent the starry sky, a reference to the secular science, particularly astronomy, taught here by Qāḍī Zāda al-Rūmī, known as the Plato of his time. Samarkand was already an important kingdom when an official of the Chinese empire discovered it in 138 BCE. This led to China learning about Europe, which in turn gave rise to the Silk Road.

Amir Temur Memorial in Samarkand

Following the Silk Road to the east, the next stop for any caravan is Bukhara, rivalling Samarkand in antiquity and importance. Bukhara's multiracial population included Jews, Afghans, Persians, Mongols as well as Hindus. In the 1920s, there were still two thousand Indians living here. They had special madrasahs and caravanserai of their own. There is a complex in Bukhara called Tokisabotan that is almost exclusively the handiwork of Indian master-builders who came north in search of work after Central Asia was conquered by the Arabs in the eleventh century.

A Russian historian in Bukhara welcomed us, remarking, 'We should continue to work together, for we are closely connected by our history through Buddhism, Islam and

The landscape of Bukhara

the Mongols. Present times connect us as well. We are glad to welcome your expedition from India as it will pave the way for future cooperation and we want to encourage this process by offering you every possible assistance.'

Bukhara was a crossroad for trade, culture and religion, especially Buddhism, Zoroastrianism, Christianity and Islam. All these left their mark on the city's architecture. And it is important for archaeologists to know this. There are Buddhist stories which suggest that caravans of Indian traders reached Central Asia as early as the third or fourth century BCE. Archaeology has shown that Bukhara has a history which goes back 2,500 years. Over this long period, the city experienced many triumphs and tragedies. The exploration of its different traditions will help the present generation discover their origins, who they are, and how their culture developed here.

Confluence of cultures in Bukhara has a long history

The name Bukhara is derived from the Sanskrit *Vihara* (Buddhist monastery). Chinese pilgrims who traversed this route between 400 and 600 CE recount Bukhara as an important Buddhist site along the trade route from India. Today Bukhara is an Islamic city. In Islam iconography is banned as only Allah should create human beings. Consequently, the focus was on calligraphy and symbolic geometrical designs which evolved into a much refined art form.

The restoration of the lost glory of Bukhara and Samarkand began in 1369 when Timur made them the foremost cities of his magnificent Central Asian Empire or Transoxiana. The great Persian poet Shiraz, known by his pen name Hafiz, mentions the two crowned jewels of Timur's empire in his poetry: 'If that naughty Turk captures my heart for the merest mole on her cheek, I would give away Samarkand and Bukhara.' Hafiz was summoned to Timur's court where an explanation was demanded of him. 'Are you aware,' said Timur, 'how difficult it was to bring Samarkand and Bukhara into our fold? How could you think of sacrificing them for a mere mole on your beloved's cheek?' Hafiz replied, 'My Lord, it is precisely for this reason that I am only a poor poet.'

The Chai corners of Bukhara

The *chaikhanas* of Bukhara fascinate me. What do the Bukharans talk about over tea? Do they still mention Hafiz and Timur? Surely they discuss current matters like break-up of the Soviet Union, market rates, and the local gossip? But I'm told, they also recount the exploits of the incomparable Mullah Nasiruddin.

Mullah Nasiruddin is an embodiment of the light-hearted, self deprecating face of Islamic mysticism. This beloved old donkey rider has been alternately referred to as a very stupid man and an incredibly clever one, and the possessor of mystical secrets. The wise Mulla, like the Sufis, aligned himself with the peasant rather than with the nobleman. His good name spread by word of mouth instead of the written word. The Mulla had scant time for the scholars who have written copiously about the heavenly preoccupations of the Sufi mystics. Indeed he playfully insists, 'I am upside-down.'

Bukhara today is a fusion of tradition and modernity

Among the many Sufi brotherhoods during Timur's reign, an important order was founded in Bukhara and came into focus under Baha-ud-Din Naqshband in the fourteenth century. It adhered to the twin mottos of finding solitude even in the midst of society and dedicating one's life to work but always keeping God in one's heart. Naqshband's tomb is one of Central Asia's most sacred sights and a popular place of pilgrimage. It is continuously attended to by Sufi dervishes, who live in the adjacent monastery and receive its visitors. Although the Naqshbandi brotherhood played a key role in the expansion of Islam in Central Asia, it incorporated stories and legends of other religions and is said to have been influenced in the beginning by Buddhism. Its main purpose was to integrate external religious rituals with inner spirituality.

Sufism took many forms. But it always involved the experience of a mystical union with God. Nowhere is this more beautifully expressed than by the whirling dervishes of Konya in Turkey. Their ecstatic trance-like dances are commonly associated with the name of another Sufi saint from Central Asia, the great thirteenth-century poet, Jalaluddin Rumi. Sufism can be traced from Central Asia to India where it flowered into mystical orders of great distinction and garnered respect from the common folk, irrespective of their caste, religion and cultural backgrounds.

In India the Mughal emperors supported and patronised the Sufis. The Mughal empire germinated with the conquest of North India in the sixteenth century and it steadily proceeded to exert authority over the entire continent in the next two centuries. Mughal

Mughal painting depicting Babur

art and architecture is among the most beautiful in the world culminating in the supreme refinement of the celebrated Taj Mahal.

The founder of the Mughal Empire was Zahir-ud-din Muhammad Babur. He was the son of a local chieftain from Andijan in Fergana Valley, south-west of Bukhara. The last great ruler of Central Asia, he was descended on his mother's side from Ghenghis Khan and on his father's side from Timur. He led his army over the Khyber Pass into India in 1525. His power rested on two major strengths – the use of gunpowder and his exceptionally fast and powerful horses.

Fergana is the legendary home of the warhorse first discovered by the Chinese traveller Chang Ch'ien, a century before the birth of Christ. Long extinct, the so-called heavenly horses have been immortalized by Han and the Tang dynasty sculptors. Despite his many years in India, Babur never forgot his beloved Fergana. The descriptions in his memoir, *Baburnama*, are so precise and detailed, that many passages still apply to what we see on our way through his homeland. He wrote lovingly of the green landscape, the many mountains and valleys, the clear streams, the profusion of fruit and flower and, of course, the many beautiful women he had married.

During Babur's time, Fergana was at the height of its prosperity – a land of abundance at the heart of the Silk Road. But after the discovery of the maritime routes, trade declined sharply. By the fifteenth century, it was already a forgotten backwater living on memories. The climate of Central Asia changed dramatically with the passing centuries and many fertile regions along the Silk Road turned into a desert wasteland. The same fate would have befallen Fergana, had it not been for a great canal built in 1939 when it was still part of the Soviet Union.

The Fergana Canal was one of the great collective efforts of that period. Sergei Eisenstein, who pictured the rousing spirit of the Russian Revolution in his film *Battleship Potemkin*, also chronicled the building of the 270 km canal. Tens of thousands of workers dug night and day to complete this vast waterway in a mere forty-five days! Fergana was preserved as the garden of Central Asia providing a rich feast for future generations. It was one of the few solid achievements of the original communist dream.

The statue of Babur at Fergana

It may have been a failed dream but I confess it was one I shared growing up in India with its abject poverty and its many superstitions, and one I would devote many years of my life to. Yet this statue of Babur strikes me as a clear proof, if one was needed, that this dream has now come to an end. Babur's statue was secretly paid for, out of funds reserved for a Lenin monument, and was brought out of hiding as soon as the Soviet Union collapsed. Ironically, it is Babur, the very symbol of India's secular heritage, who now provides an Islamic identity for the new nation of Uzbekistan.

On the twelfth day of our journey, we crossed the border between the newly created nations of Uzbekistan and Kyrgyzstan. The two former states of the Soviet Union seem unfamiliar with the formalities of visas and passports and simply wave us off.

Unfolding before my eyes are the forgotten images of my childhood. Here are the wandering minstrels calling us to the ancient host country of the Kyrgyz nomads … here once more the tartars of the golden horde galloping across the steppes. Here where *Taras Bulbas* reigned and Ghenghis Khan conquered – where man invented the saddle and the stirrup and a culture that would briefly dominate the world – the pages of my favourite storybooks come to life again. I see the legendary children who learn to ride before they can walk and whose mothers still make *kumis*, the hard liquor that comes from mare's milk. And I remember how I once wished to be one of them. Recalling the fabled history

Lunch at Fergana

of this land, as its mountains continue to rise up before us, I find it hard to believe that this was once the driving heart of Asia.

There are similar places in the Indian foothills of the Himalayas where droplets from a cascading stream can resonate forever, and the ripples of the shepherd's flock dictate the silent rhythms of the valley. Yet familiar landscapes do not make for understanding the Himalayan barrier, and the colonial politics of the last 200 years make me a stranger here. What hopes or dreams, what underlying values do I share with the people of Kyrgyzstan? And yet, the tempo of daily life and the old ways of this nomadic society strike a chord of sympathy in my heart.

Osh Bazaar

Bishkek, the capital of Kyrgyzstan, is a modern city built in the 1930s. It has a cosmopolitan air about it. People flock to its market from all the surrounding regions. Here Kazakhs, Ukrainians and Uzbeks mingle with visitors from faraway places like Azerbaijan and Mongolia. Here is even a community of Korean immigrants. However, the largest sector of the population is Russian.

The market is called the Osh Bazaar and takes its name from an ancient Silk Road market town. As the word *bazaar* implies, it is more than a shopping centre. It is a Central Asian crossroad where people of different nationalities gather and where the histories of their struggles with each other can be read in their contrasting features.

Kyrgyzstan, like her neighbours, is a fragile multi-ethnic republic with a brand new market economy. Before coming to Central Asia, we had read that food was scarce and people did not have enough to eat. But we find the markets overflowing with fruits and flowers, meat and vegetables, all at reasonable prices. Yet I cannot help wondering

A Kyrgyz family

whether Osh Bazaar will survive the onslaught of modern times with its regional rivalries, new mafias and consumer pressures. What will the future hold for these splendid people now that the ideals of old communist orders have so clearly failed them? With more questions than answers, we head towards the Tien Shan mountains and back in the nomad country.

Many Kyrgyz nomads converted to Islam only in the eighteenth century, much later than the people of the cities. Their folk history is a mixture of Shamanism and the earlier religions of the Silk Road. Kyrgyzstan has a multilayered history, each layer resting on the one below it like geological strata. But the newest layer, the top soil, is a multi-ethnic one. The Islamic Kyrgyz now share their land with more than a million Russian orthodox Christians, the most recent immigrants to this age-old cauldron of Asia. Kyrgyzstan has reverted to being an Islamic republic. But the reality is clearly more complex. Can this new nation really succeed without bringing all its people under a single banner?

Views around Lake Issyk-Kul

High up in the Tien Shan mountains at a height of 5,600 ft is Lake Issyk-Kul, the warm lake. It is so called because the water's high salt content prevents it from freezing, even in winter. This inland sea extends for 114 miles and has long served as a resting place for the weary Silk Road traveller. The famous Chinese pilgrim Xuanzang wrote of sea dragons and dark rolling waves endlessly lapping the shore. The local people were shepherds and no one dared to fish in the lake. If a sea monster was sighted, it was

The vestige of Lenin

considered an omen and travellers then prayed for good fortune. Xuanzang might have been pleased to see one of these monsters for he had reached the lake after a bitter mountain crossing during which a third of his caravan had died from starvation and cold.

Despite its legendary monster, Lake Issyk-Kul seems to me a paradise waiting to be discovered and all the more alluring for being as yet untouched. When Xuanzang passed by thirteen centuries ago, it was a summering camp for the great Khan of the Western Turks. But his hundred thousand warriors made no permanent impression on the landscape. Will future generations be able to say the same of us? I wonder …

Statues depicting the Silk Route

The descendants of the great Mughal Khans continue to ride their steeds from dawn to dusk. Cowboys have almost disappeared from the American West but here in Central Asia they still herd their cattle as they have done since time immemorial. They contemplate their fields and mountains at the end of a long day's work oblivious to the march of history and the new troubled relationship between man and nature. Bactrian camels roam freely in the field beside the road. These double-humped camels were the mainstay of ancient caravans along the eastern end of the Silk Road. Each one could carry up to sixty pounds for twenty miles a day on little food or water. Their sense of smell alone saved countless lives, helping them find water by faint whips of greenery on the wind. I don't know what practical use camels could have today but I am thrilled at my first sight of these free-roaming herds. I don't even bother to ask.

Our jeep climbed all day until we reached the 8,300 ft Dolon Pass in the Tien Shan or Heavenly Mountains. It is cold even in June. On the other side of the Dolon Pass lies the last stretch of road between Kyrgyzstan and China. We have already passed through the token checkpoints of three countries, all of them former republics of the Soviet Union. Now we are approaching a real border. On the far side of the next mountain range is the Peoples' Republic of China.

The first leg of our journey is drawing to a close. In my mind's eye, the map of Central Asia is no longer blank. It is being filled with the wealth of new images, many unbearably fleeting, and I wonder if I am any the wiser for them. All blanks have been filled only to open up new ones. Knowing what I do not know, there is an urge to remain and learn more. Yet, I've been bitten by the traveller's disease and I am eager to move on to new adventures.

I used to think of the great nations to the north of us, as somehow swimming in the mainstream of history with India left far behind, paralyzed by the deep routes of its enclosed culture. Now I am less sure. On this side of the mountain I see only more little worlds, different from mine but equally routed and self-enclosed. I am reminded once more of Mullah Nasiruddin. 'What time is it in Central Asia?' I hear myself ask and then Nasiruddin's reply, 'Couldn't tell you, I am a stranger here myself.'

The statue of Mullah Nasiruddin

Entry to China

On the way to Kashgar Bazaar

IN SEARCH OF THE BUDDHA

Like any storyteller returning from a long journey, I spent the months following our expedition attempting to give shape to a series of images, thoughts and feelings. The pieces of film were my notes, waiting for a viewpoint to give them life.

An expedition of this kind is made up of many private journeys, each adding a different perspective to the whole. I decided to see the second episode as Michael's story. A Western Buddhist on the trail of an ancient Chinese pilgrim who made a famous pilgrimage to India in search of the Buddha.

The cart road to Kashgar

MICHAEL'S STORY:

Our first stop was the ancient oasis known to the Chinese as Kashi, but more frequently as Kashgar by the local Uighur population. An old nomadic tribe, the Uighurs have been living along the Silk Road for over two thousand years. They share racial and cultural roots with their Turkic neighbours to the West. One gets the feeling of travelling into the distant past upon arriving at Kashgar.

However, Kashgar was once a thriving centre with its strategic location on the Silk route. Even today the great Sunday bazaar attracts farmers from the countryside and neighbouring oases. The empty carts stand idle by the Tuman river as their owners line the bridge and the streets of old Kashgar with their wares.

The first impression of the bazaar is that of a large flea market along the lines found in India or even in some Western cities. Interestingly enough, there used to be a well-known flea bazaar here, named after the area of the market that traded in old clothes.

So Kashgar may well have been the original model for a flea market.

What really drew us to the bazaar were the people. Here was a place where buying and selling and general entertainments are all of a piece. A strange amalgam of the old and the new, the market keeps surprising us by alternating between the exotic and the mundane.

The *chaikhana* or tea shop has its roots in antiquity. But in former times, a

The faces of Kashgar

mandolin player or a storyteller would have held his audience spellbound rather than Chinese cartoons. I have been waiting in Kashgar for the arrival of the rest of the team, assessing the price of pigeons at the bird market.

Michael with the sparrow

How much? Three yuan?

I finally buy a sparrow, but its wing has been clipped. So I guess it will have to sit on my shoulder until I can find someone who wants a pet bird rather than a Chinese supper.

~

Kashgar Bazaar

Kashgar Bazaar (continued)

Kashgar Bazaar (continued)

Kashgar Bazaar (continued)

Kashgar Bazaar (continued)

Kashgar Bazaar (continued)

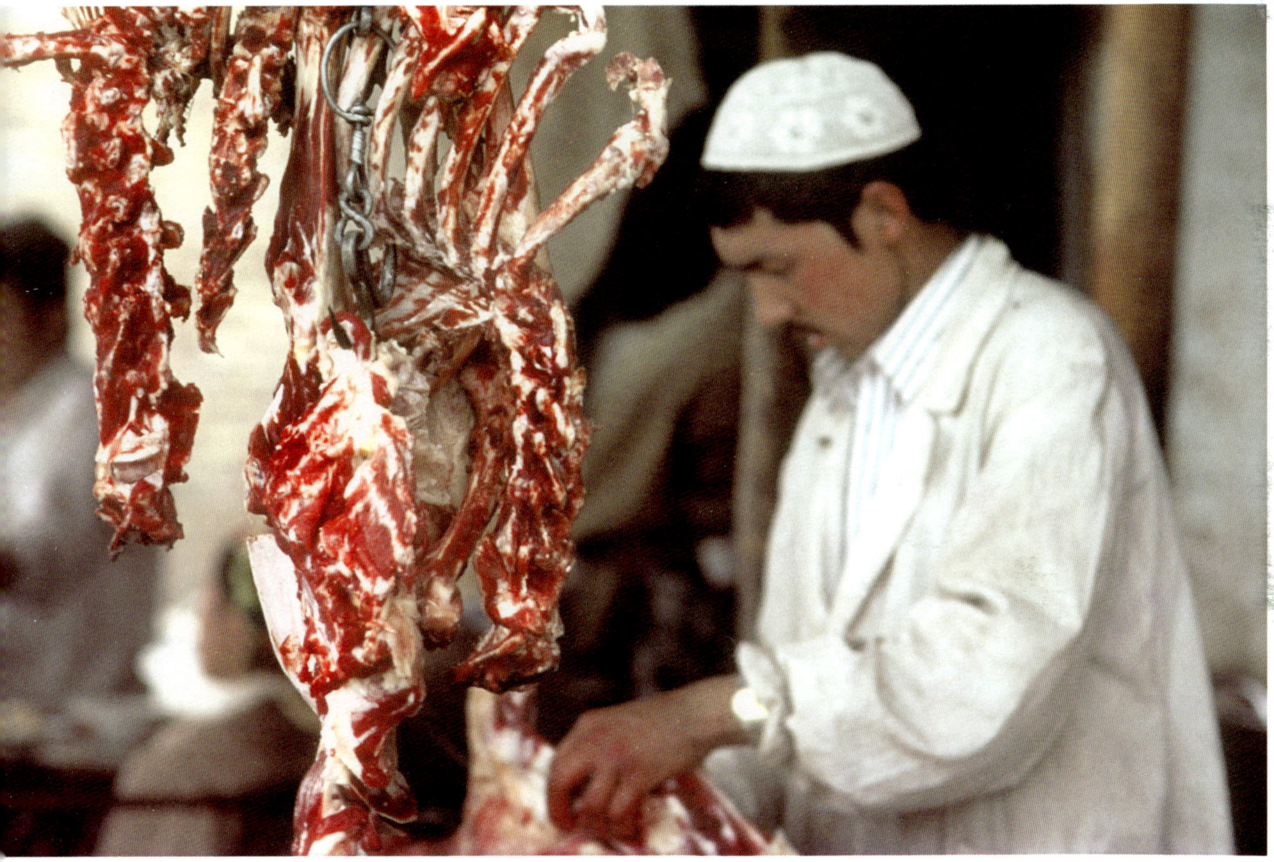

Kashgar Bazaar (continued)

Kashgar Bazaar (continued)

Kashgar Bazaar (continued)

Scenes from Kashgar

Scenes from Kashgar (continued)

Scenes from Kashgar (continued)

Scenes from Kashgar (continued)

Michael with Hari in Chini-bagh

A hundred years ago, there were better buys to be had in the Kashgar Bazaar than sparrows. George McCartney, the lone British representative in this remote corner of Asia, bought some souvenirs that were to startle the world. I visited Chini-bagh, the residence of George McCartney with Hari. Hari and I are deep in conversation. 'We are walking exactly where it all began, where they found the very first manuscript that made Central Asia such an incredible place for all the art historians, excavators and explorers.'

Left: Old photograph of Kashgar; Right: Lord George McCartney and Lady Catherine McCartney

Hari replies, 'When Eric Shipton came to my house, I think in the 70s, he spoke of this place, as though speaking of a dream. It excited me and I wondered if ever I would be here, and see we are here today!'

~

At the turn of the century, Chini-bagh, as the British Consulate was called, served as a strategic listening post beyond the Himalayas with British India in its cold war against the rapidly expanding Russian Empire.

I went to the British Museum and then I read about Aurel Stein, Sven Hedin and Le Coq. They all talked about Chini-bagh and Lady McCartney's Garden and I thought this must be the most remote and romantic place in the world. I never thought I'd actually be walking here.

In her memoir of Chini-bagh, *An English Lady in Chinese Turkestan* (1931), Lady McCartney recounts how it became the most famous guesthouse in Central Asia.

Marc Aurel Stein

My husband acquired a quantity of broken pottery, stone and metal seals, and stucco, figurines of Buddha, and some 35 leaves of manuscript from native 'treasure seekers', evidently picked up by them in the desert.

He looked upon his acquisitions as mere curios; nevertheless he sent them to Professor Hoernle, a well-known Sanskrit scholar. What was his surprise when the Professor wrote to tell him that these manuscripts were the oldest Indian hand-written documents then known to exist! They were of the fourth century AD.

Many scientific expeditions came in consequence, the most important of them being those of our friends Sir Aurel Stein and the late Professor Albert von Le Coq. They excavated a great number of ruined sights around the Taklamakan Desert – often at several days march from any present-day habitation.

If any of my readers think I am making too much of the past cultural importance of Turkestan, let him or her go to the British Museum and ask for the Stein Collection.

A civilization had emerged full-blown from the desert, linking for the first time the four great cultures of the ancient world: Greece, Persia, India and China. Stein called it Serindia. His chief source of clues was the travel diary of the seventh-century Buddhist pilgrim called

Left: Aurel Stein collection, British Musuem

A Statue of Xuanzang

Xuanzang. Marc Aurel Stein was born in Budapest in 1862. A unique combination of scholar, explorer and archaeologist, he conducted one of the greatest raids on the ancient world that has ever been attempted.

Our local guide escorts us to one of the ancient sites described by Xuanzang called Mor Temple. It was part of a Tang dynasty town where the pilgrim stopped on his return from India. There, along the ramparts, is the stupa of Mor Temple, an adored tower that once held a niche for the Buddha image. Before his arrival, Xuanzang had narrowly escaped death at the hands of bandits. Did he, right here, bow to the Buddha and offer thanks for his deliverance?

The next morning we set off across the desert toward Yarkand, the next oasis town over two hundred miles away. It is our first taste of the heat and glare and dust of the Taklamakan which in Turkic means 'he who goes in does not come out'. From the comparative comfort of our jeep, I think of Xuanzang and Marc Aurel Stein, travelling this same route when there was nothing but the bleached bones of dead men and animals to mark their way.

Yarkand is an oasis with orchards, fields and poplar-lined roads stretching seventy or eighty miles along the southern Silk Road. It seems almost untouched by the present century. Yarkand has been forgotten by history. The old caravanserai on Kashmir Street could be waiting for the Silk Road traders to arrive laden with gold and spices from India.

Left: The Taklamakan desert; Right: A stupa at Mor Temple

And I can imagine Stein refitting his footsore animals here before setting off in search of buried cities.

Stein's caravan left Yarkand in December 1900. It was the first of his three great expeditions, spanning a period of sixteen years. Following Xuanzang's clues, he excavated a succession of ancient sites. They had exotic names like Miran, Kandalik and Loulan and yielded a stream of remarkable relics. His success sparked an international race for the buried treasures of Chinese Turkestan. An ancient civilization preserved in the sand offered up its secrets by the ton.

Aurel Stein's photographs of excavations in Taklamakan desert

Nearly a century later, Chinese archaeologists continue to find new evidence of one of their earliest cultures. But they are the latecomers. By 1930, a whole chapter of history had already been carted off to foreign lands. Stein was branded a foreign devil who had stolen China's past and he was refused permission to conduct a fourth expedition. Stein died in 1943 with his discoveries safely locked away in the British Museum. The man himself was conveniently forgotten.

There is one place, however, where he is still given credit for his achievements: India's National Museum in Delhi. The British Raj co-funded Stein's expeditions and were entitled to half of everything he found. As a result, India inherited an impressive collection of Central Asian art. And in these rooms Serindia finally comes to life for me. Stein's discovery of such lost languages as Karoshti, Sogdian and Brahmi show how the once vibrant Buddhist culture of Central Asia had spread from India, and how it evolved after coming into contact with Chinese, Persian and Ancient Greek cultures along the Silk Road. The art, literature and artifacts he brought back are among the earliest examples anywhere in the world. Stein was a brilliant Orientalist. He turned to exploration to confirm his theories on the evolution of ancient Buddhist culture.

Recalling his discoveries, my heart skips a beat as we approach our first sand-buried city. Twenty-two miles south of present-day Khotan is the ancient capital of Melikawat. Aside from the chance for a little unexpected exercise, it is a disappointment. In 1977, the Chinese are supposed to have dug up an imperial hall and a collection of Tang dynasty pottery here. But all I can see are bits of old wall which might easily be mistaken for boulders. It is the desert wind that really fires my imagination, the same dry wind that suddenly swallowed up an entire epoch.

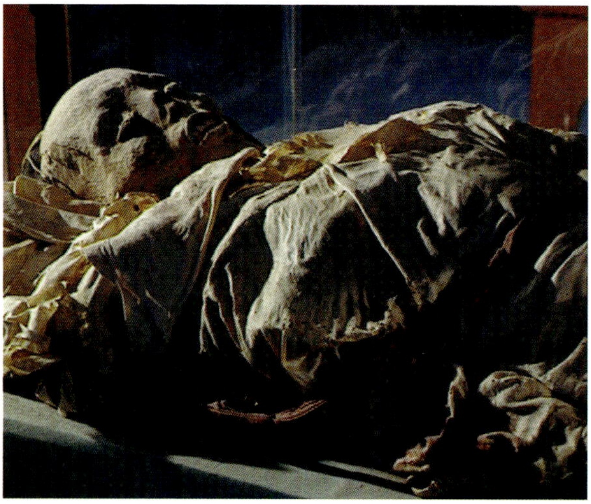

Preserved mummy at Khotan musuem

~

In a small museum at Khotan, Goutam filmed some mummified bodies preserved in sarcophagi. There are bodies buried in the sand, remaining intact for thousands of years. A woman looks as though she was almost alive. 'Where did she come from?'

The keeper replies, 'They are from the sixth century.'

I am astonished. 'Sixth century! That means this woman has been buried in the sand just like she is for 1,400 years, with her shoes on and her clothes just as they are and hair perfectly intact. It's extraordinary! And this is her nine-year-old daughter. See her hair. Were they Buddhist?'

'Yes, they are Buddhist.'

'That's amazing.'

It's like looking at Xuanzang and thinking about the journey that he undertook from China to India to pick up the manuscripts. Here are real people from his time perfectly preserved. It's fantastic.

The caves of Kirk Makan

The meditation caves of Kirk Makan overlook the Karakash river. Over time followers of different faiths have found refuge here. Just when I thought that the trail of Xuanzang had gone cold, and there was nothing more to learn about him, the Silk Road has begun to offer us new insights.

Xuanzang was inspired by Fa-hsien, a third-century pilgrim. The Buddhist scriptures found in this cave belong to Fa-hsien's time. It is difficult to imagine that the scriptures lay here undisturbed for nearly 1,700 years. The peaceful tranquility here at Kirk Makan gives us a glimpse of eternity. There are few distractions; no sense of time rushing by.

Praying within the caves of Kirk Makan

On the spot where a Nestorian monk would have prayed to Jesus, or a Chinese pilgrim meditated, a Muslim woman now invokes the name of Allah. Prayer beads are an ancient aid to meditation, used in each of these spiritual traditions. Counting beads is a way of emptying the mind of disturbing thoughts, the first step in any spiritual training. A clear mind, it is said, produces a calm heart and death itself can be faced without fear.

If sand is the messenger of death, water is the angel of life in the desert. When there is no rainfall, water is more precious than gold. Everything requires water, even the houses. Courtyards and mud-brick walls need to be washed down every day or the dry air will quickly reduce them to dust. On this daily water-giving ritual rests the entire history of civilization along the Silk Road.

We arrive to find families harvesting their apricots. And my interpreter and I are invited to pick our own basketful of fruit. I asked her if we should offer to pay, but Guli

– whose name means desert flower – says it would be insulting. This is how the Uighurs see us off along the Silk Road.

In the small country villages outside Khotan, oral traditions survive which preserve the memory of the Silk Road in a very vivid way. The head of this village is a well-known *nagara* drummer who relives the history he heard as a child in the songs and lyrics he now performs for others.

The storyteller at Khotan

'Can you tell me the story about Xuanzang and the nagara? I believe the king of Khotan arranged for singing, dancing and merry-making and himself played a similar instrument for Xuanzang.'

The nagara player answers eagerly, 'An ancient instrument, the nagara has been passed down to successive generations. The king used the nagara to communicate important information to his people – be it a festival or an accident or an urgent matter. The sound of the nagara brought people together.'

Some locals claim to have heard the sound of drums beating in the temple of the nagara at night. It was a sanctuary for many Buddhist priests. In ancient times, it would have been called the 'Temple of the Ghanta' after the drum that called monks and laymen to prayer. In his diary Xuanzang recounts the legend which gave the temple its name.

In the days before Buddhism came to Central Asia a king discovered a disciple of Buddha in deep meditation. Hearing of the man who had conquered birth and death, the king wanted the Buddha to appear before him. The disciple told him to build a temple on this spot. The king complied and then asked again to see the Buddha. The disciple replied that if the king exercised true faith then he will appear. At that moment there descended from the air a figure of the Buddha who confirmed the king's faith and gave him a ghanta drum for his temple. This is how the collective memory of an ancient race is passed down through the generations by word of mouth.

Leaving the main expedition for a few days, we fly to Xi'an in the heartland of China. The Silk Road ends here among the rice paddies of Shaanxi province. In Xuanzang's time, these fields lay within the walled city of Chang'an, the imperial capital during the Tang dynasty. The tombs of the Tang emperors are grouped on a hillside outside Xi'an. A party of headless ambassadors, known only by the foreign names on their backs, reflects the cosmopolitan flavour of an era that represents the best in Chinese art and culture.

In the seventh century, Chang'an was the gateway for all the new ideas arriving along the Silk Road. In the market quarter of Xi'an, a modern statue commemorates the starting point of the ancient caravan route. Traders brought their goods here from Central Asia and beyond, exchanging them for iron, gold, silk and the newly popular tea. The Bell Tower stands at the centre of the Tang dynasty city where Xuanzang returned after his 10,000 mile pilgrimage to India and back.

Wild Goose Pagoda in the Temple of Great Goodwill

Although Xi'an is a major industrial centre, its historic sites attract tourists from around the world. Today its two million inhabitants are no greater in number than they were in the year 1645 when Xuanzang's caravan arrived laden with books, images and holy relics. The people of Chang'an had heard of his incredible voyage to distant, far-off places and they poured out of their houses to welcome the Buddhist master whose adventures had already become legendary. Xuanzang is a folk hero in China and his Wild Goose Pagoda in the Temple of Great Goodwill is a famous landmark. The emperor T'ai-tsung built Xuanzang this stone tower to house his manuscripts. Here the pilgrim spent the last years of his life translating them with a team of hand-picked scholars. The new corpus of Buddhist teachings was destined to have an immense impact on all the cultures of the Far East.

Moved by the reverence still shown to this remarkable man, I pay my own respects in the traditional manner.

Emperor T'ai-tsung was a Confucian and had been hostile to Buddhism as a young man, but in his later years he took a deep interest in this new religion. Xuanzang became the emperor's spiritual advisor and used his influence to strengthen the position of Buddhism in China. During the Tang dynasty, new and distinctly Chinese forms of Buddhism emerged. Xuanzang's own sect lasted a mere seventy years after his death. But his translations influenced many schools which have survived to this day, including the famous Chán school which travelled to Japan where it became known as Zen.

The Temple of the Flourishing Teaching is a seventh-century monastery to the south of Xi'an. Its monks and lay followers still chant the original Sanskrit verses brought back from India by Xuanzang, and honour his memory by circling the tower that holds his ashes. Inscribed on his tomb is the word *Tripitika*, or three-fold basket, which refers to the original core of Buddhist Teaching.

Tripitika became the nickname for Xuanzang. At twenty-seven he set out on his pilgrimage and did not return until he was forty-three. Unconvinced by the translations then available in China, he sought the true teachings of the Buddha in the holy land of India. He walked alone into the great unknown, crossing the world's greatest deserts, and its highest mountain ranges. He faced death many times, and his courage and equanimity impressed kings, bandits and barbarians alike. He lectured at monasteries and debated with learned monks and by the time he reached his destination, his reputation as a great sage had already preceded him. Xuanzang was not the only Chinese pilgrim to visit the homeland of Buddhism, but he was the most important. Like a dead star that keeps releasing energy for thousands of years, he continues to be a valuable source of knowledge and inspiration.

~

The modern state of Bihar in India contains the principal sites where the Buddha lived and taught during his lifetime. With the decline of Buddhism in India, these sites were either destroyed or abandoned. Many centuries would pass before archaeologists

Bodh Gaya before Independence courtesy of Bourne and Shepherd

Bodh Gaya today

and art historians would seek them out again. And like Aurel Stein, they would invariably turn to Xuanzang to guide their footsteps.

A short distance from the present city of Gaya lies Bodh Gaya, where the Buddha is said to have achieved Enlightenment. This most sacred of sites is once again a centre for pilgrims from all the different Buddhist countries of the Far East. Western tourists mingle with visitors from Bhutan, Southeast Asia, Japan and, of course, Tibet.

A few months after the expedition is over, my wife and I arrive in India to see where Xuanzang's long pilgrimage had led him.

'We are coming round to the Bodhi tree just around the corner here. There it is. You can recognize it by its leaves. You've seen it in some of the pictures.'

Katherine, my wife, exclaims, 'Oh, it's beautiful! Look at the size of it!'

'This is the fourth Bodhi tree. It was brought from Sri Lanka by Sir Alexander Cunningham, the archaeologist who uncovered this place in the late nineteenth century,' I inform her.

'What a marvellous tree! Amazing how big it's become.'

'These are the Buddha's footsteps. See how they are painted red, saffron-coloured. Little coins are put here as offerings. Before the Gandara period, there was no Buddha image and so the only image of Buddha was the wheel of life, the fish that was one of his thirty-two marks of a great man … and his footsteps.'

Statue of Buddha

The Buddha was an Indian prince called Siddhartha Goutama, who renounced a life of luxury and privilege for that of a wandering ascetic. Confronted with the bitter reality of life outside his palace gates, he asked whether there could be a way to end all suffering. The beggar women and children at the temple gates are a constant reminder of this pertinent question. The Buddha was concerned with more than the alleviation of physical poverty. He came to see suffering as the basic human condition, as universal as old age, sickness and death. It was not a matter of living a sheltered life or even of extending that opportunity to as many people as possible. The burning issue that made him leave his palace and seek an answer was much deeper. And the more he meditated on it the more elusive the answer seemed. He studied with the best teachers of his age. For six years, he imposed the most severe hardships on himself until he was emaciated and on the point of death. Yet there was no solution to his problem so he gave up his austerities and nourished

Buddhist iconography

himself until his body was strong again. Then he sat down beneath the Bodhi tree for one final supreme effort, vowing not to get up until he was fully enlightened.

Not far from Bodh Gaya is a peaceful valley that seems to have changed very little from the time the Buddha walked there 2,500 years ago. Having reached the end of his ascetic life, the Buddha bathed in a nearby river.

'This is truly one of the most beautiful places that I have ever seen.'

Katherine says, 'Wonderful. I just loved watching the little child and the mother putting all the wheat in a big bushel and the child playing with it and making a little hat out of it. Everywhere there are children and animals. It has stopped in time. It's just the way the Buddha must have seen it 2,500 years ago. But the world really has changed … Where is the river?'

'Just over there. That's where the Buddha met Sujata.'

'Sujata, the young girl who gave him a bowl of milk. And what was the story?'

'This must be where he came when he was doing his real privations and he was starving and very emaciated and he came and sat by the riverbed, didn't he?'

'That's right. And a shepherd looked after him.'

'And a shepherd looked after him and then a shepherd girl came with a bowl of milk.'

'And that was Sujata. Well, this is still … Sujata's valley.'

Alone among the world's great teachers the Buddha never claimed to be more than a human being. His teaching mission lasted forty-five years and would yield an enormous body of work. But he summed it up in a single phrase: 'Suffering I teach, and the way out of suffering.'

One of his first monastic orders was started in a mango grove at Nalanda, later to become the greatest university in Asia. It is the largest of all ancient Buddhist centres and a must for any tourist making a tour of sacred sites. Xuanzang spent many months in Nalanda and gives a glowing description of its attractions: lecture halls, libraries, temples and flower gardens and, above all, the greatest Buddhist teachers of the day.

Katherine exclaims, 'The place is so well preserved. It's like Pompei.'

'Yes, there must have been about ten thousand monks living here at the time of Xuanzang.'

'Do you think he slept in one of these?'

'It could be. I doubt whether these were the exact same walls. It was rediscovered by Cunningham in the twentieth century and a lot of things were rebuilt.'

'Didn't you tell me Xuanzang's teachers had a dream about his coming?'

'Yes, a portent. Shilabhadra was the teacher. He was a famous Mahayana teacher and he lived here and taught here. He was the master of Nalanda and he lived in great pain. He had terrible arthritis and one time it was so bad he wanted to simply waste away. And he had this terribly powerful dream which told him not to do such a thing. And that he was going to be the master of a very important Chinese pilgrim. And this pilgrim was going to ask him for the Mahayana teachings.'

'And it was Xuanzang.'

'And when Xuanzang arrived and actually came up to him and said, *My name is Xuanzang and I want the teachings of the Mahayana* – at that time it was called the Yogachara teachings – *and I want you to be my teacher* … Shilabhadra looked up to him and wept.'

60

So a crucial transmission took place that would help ensure the smooth passage of Buddhism to China and beyond. Buddhism soon disappeared from India and the timeliness of Xuanzang's pilgrimage became apparent to all. He had followed in the footsteps of the Buddha in the holy land and within his own heart. He was one of the world's great travellers, but his journey, like that of the Buddha, was principally an inward one. A true disciple, Xuanzang strove earnestly to liberate his own heart and in so doing, became himself a light for others to follow.

Light and warmth are two aspects of the liberated humanised energy. Hence the Buddha is called both the all-enlightened one with the single-eyed wisdom and the all-compassionate one with the heart that radiates love. The Buddha never encouraged blind faith or belief in anything that could not be experienced firsthand. The liberated warmth from his heart shone forth encouraging others to break through their self-delusions and awaken to their true nature. For those inclined to follow him, he taught a middle way between self-indulgence and self-mortification. But the Buddha did not promise deliverance. He said he could only point the way. Everyone had to walk each step of their way like the great pilgrim Xuanzang on their own two feet.

Jataka tale carved in stone

A mural at Mogao Caves

A TALE OF THE SILK ROUTE

This is our 26th day on the road and the start of the third leg of the journey. The northern arm of the Silk Road hugs the foothills of the Tien Shan mountains on the edge of the Taklamakan desert. Until the Chinese tarmacked the road in 1970, it was just a dirt track which at night or in a sandstorm became a trackless wilderness.

The first European to map this desolate region was the Swedish explorer Sven Hedin. His first expedition in 1895 was very nearly his last. The local guide supplied enough water for four days in the desert, instead of the ten requested. When the caravan lost its way, the guide was the first to die. The others became insane with thirst, drinking anything – even sheep's blood and camel's urine. By the fifth day, the men, camels and other livestock were all dead except for Sven Hedin and one other man.

Sven Hedin

Hedin writes in *Through Asia* (1995), 'If I was doomed to die in the sand, I wanted to be properly attired; I wanted my burial clothes to be both white and clean.' But fate was on his side. Spying the dark green line of an oasis, he dragged himself to safety. 'I stood on the brink of a little pool filled with fresh, cool water-beautiful water! I drank, drank, drank time after time ... every blood-vessel and tissue of my body sucked up the-life-giving liquid like a sponge.'

Sven Hedin at work

Sven Hedin went on to explore the Taklamakan and Gobi deserts as no man had done before him. He discovered the first sand-buried city which the archaeologist Marc Aurel Stein would later excavate.

By nightfall we reach our first campsite. The local fishing community of Lake Bachu gives a feast in our honour. A lake in the desert, freshly caught fish, ancient pentatonic music … and a raging fire create a primeval atmosphere.

As the ancient Chinese empire expanded westward year by year, a line of watchtowers were built to protect the Silk Road caravans from marauding tribes. One of the last surviving towers stands near the oasis of Kucha. Built in the third century CE, its original wooden struts have been miraculously preserved by the dry desert air. Hidden in the bluff overlooking the oasis are the caves of Kyzil Kara. They were carved into the rock face between the third and the tenth century when Buddhism was still the dominant religion of Central Asia. The caves contained small cells for monks to sleep and meditate in, and larger ones for group study and chanting.

Left and Middle: Albert von Le Coq at the excavation site; Right: Paul Pelliot at work

When the Chinese pilgrim Xuanzang passed through Kucha, it was an independent kingdom with its own language, music and painting. At Kyzil, the French archaeologist Paul Pelliot discovered Buddhist documents on birch bark that turned out to be the first evidence of the lost Kuchean language, a variant of the Indian Sanskrit. But the man who really made his name here was a tough German doctor called Albert von Le Coq.

Greco-Buddhist art arose at the time of Alexander the Great, whose Greek army reached as far as the Peshawar valley, now in Pakistan. The classic meditating Buddha was a Greek inspiration. It broke from the early Indian tradition of representing the Buddha only with symbols. Ironically, this Hellenistic imagery provoked Muslim conquerors into destroying Buddhist art which they regarded as idolatry and an offense against Allah. But Le Coq discovered another reason: 'The belief exists that painted men and animals, unless their eyes and mouths at least had been destroyed, come to life at night, descend from their places, and do all sorts of mischief to men, beasts and harvests' (*Buried Treasures of Chinese Turkestan*).

From left to right: Tower at Kucha; Uighur children at Kucha and Uighur madrasahs

The artistic Kucheans were gradually absorbed by the Uighurs, a Turkic tribe who converted to Islam in the tenth century. Like other Muslims, they learn their Koran in madrasahs, the traditional Islamic schools. The Uighurs are Chinese citizens but culturally they occupy the eastern fringe of an Islamic civilization that stretches right across Asia and North Africa.

~

Aksu is a modern town with a large population of Han Chinese immigrants. It is our first taste of China proper, but it seems strangely out of place in this desert setting. Over the centuries, China's borders have ebbed and flowed like a tide. In 1949, it reasserted control over Chinese Turkestan, renaming it Xinjiang province. The first wholesale transfer of Han Chinese to the new province was ordered by Chairman Mao. The children of these latter-day pioneers are the second generation to grow up there. Beyond Aksu, Uighur cowboys drive their horses and cattle to the market … and camera-toting tourists look like aliens from a future century.

A school at Kucha

Lunch is a quick pit stop at a Chinese café, but this is fast food with a difference. Meat and vegetables are kept raw until ordered, and even the noodles are made on the spot. Legend has it that spaghetti was brought back from China by Marco Polo. If so, he may have tasted this new dish at a caravan stop like this one.

The heat and dust and the long distances between one oasis and another make for a gruelling trip, even in the jeep. The restaurant signs may only be in Uighur or Chinese but they are always a welcome sight. There are several hundred miles to cover each day we are on the road. For long stretches, there is nothing for the eye to contemplate but a ribbon of black tar between an endless expanse of desert and sky. Only our Chinese hosts know where we are going and how long it should take us to get there, barring unforeseen mishaps. The wind blows a continuous stream of sand grit and small stones against our cars and some are as sharp as bullets. When a windscreen bursts on one of our jeeps, bits of glass spray everywhere. Whatever happens to a vehicle has to be repaired on the spot. And time and again we thank Gavin, our quiet mechanic, who gets us going again.

Ruins at Yarkhoto

Yarkhoto stands on a high cliff surrounded by riverbeds. It was already the capital of a Han dynasty province in 200 BCE. The Chinese took refuge here from the same early Huns who drove the emperor to build the Great Wall of China. The layout of a later Tang dynasty town still survives.

In the nineteenth century the Russian botanist Dmitri Klementz explored Yarkhoto and other nearby sites. He took pictures, drew ground plans and removed the first temple murals. He published a report showing the precise location of each site. But the Russians did not return to Central Asia until four years later. By then, the path had been well-trodden by others. Armed with the Russian's map, Le Coq set out from Urumqi in September 1904.

Today Urumqi is an industrial city, the capital of Xinjiang province. It lies further from the sea than any other city in the world and its name means 'Beautiful Pastures'. And a short drive away we find one of the great beauty spots of Central Asia. To discover

Heaven's Lake

Heaven's Lake after weeks in the desert is strangely liberating. That's our Hormuzd in a Uighur cap, and Akhil hanging off the boat. But they're not the only ones in high spirits. It's a place for a bit of fantasy and fun. Tourists have fun by sitting on a chained live horse.

More convincing descendants of the Mongol king are camped only a few miles away. Kazakh nomads have roamed these parts since ancient times. Like the Mongols, they live in portable yurts and depend on their horses and livestock for a living. As a minority people, they are allowed larger families than the Han Chinese who are restricted to only one child per couple. Milk, cheese and meat form the basis of their diet.

Their freedom and self-sufficiency is enviable, at least to those of us who have grown up in a

Various moods of Kazak nomads

big city. But the days of nomads and camel caravans on the Silk Road are over. They are more of a tourist attraction than a real part of the region's economy. A constant stream of trucks carries raw materials and supplies between modern trading centres like Aksu and Urumqi. Aerodynamic windmills, factories and trains give their true taste of the future, reawakened China growing at an astonishing rate of fifteen per cent a year and about to become an industrial giant. We follow the train across lush green fields lined with poplar trees. These fields are fed by the cold mountain streams of the Tien Shan or Heavenly Mountains which divides the desert basin from the steps of Mongolia.

We begin our descent to the Turpan basin, also known as the Land of Fire. At 300 feet below sea level, the changes in climate are extreme. The winters are freezing cold and the summers are so hot that people build houses underground. The oasis of Turpan has a highly efficient irrigation system called the *karez*. Developed over 2,000 years ago, it is an elaborate network of underground channels fed by glaciers and linked to a series of wells. The karez system uses gravity to bring water to the surface, often at a great distance from its original source. And people of the oasis depend on it for their survival. If the karez was neglected, the oasis would soon shrivel up and die. But properly maintained, it provides an abundance of crops, including wheat, cotton, melons and the best grapes in this part of the world. Dubbed 'mare's nipple' because of their oval shapes, these grapes provided the first wine to be drunk in China during the Tang dynasty.

Tuyoq is famous for its fine vineyards. It lies in the gorge beneath the Flaming Mountains. In 1905, Le Coq discovered fourth-century Buddhist caves in the red sandstone hills above the town. Over the centuries, holy men continue to use them as meditation treats and today Tuyoq is a place of pilgrimage in Central Asia.

We don't see many pilgrims, but there are plenty of children around. In summer, Uighur families live in open-air courtyards. They use their flat roofs for drying grapes or growing vegetables. The pace of life is as slow as you would expect in the hottest place on the surface of the earth.

South of Tuyoq lie the ruins of Karakhoja built as a garisson town in the second century BCE. It became the capital of the kingdom of Gaochang during the Han dynasty. In the ninth century, the Uighurs built their kingdom of Karakhoja here. They introduced the Manichaean religion which flourished alongside Buddhism and Christianity.

Le Coq reached Karakhoja on 18 November 1905. Much of the city had been destroyed by local farmers who regarded the old walls with their brightly painted frescoes as an excellent fertilizer. Carved temple beams were also carted off to be used as firewood.

Then a farmer led Le Coq to what he later described as his greatest single achievement – a ninth-century fresco of what he spoke to be the prophet Mani surrounded by his disciples.

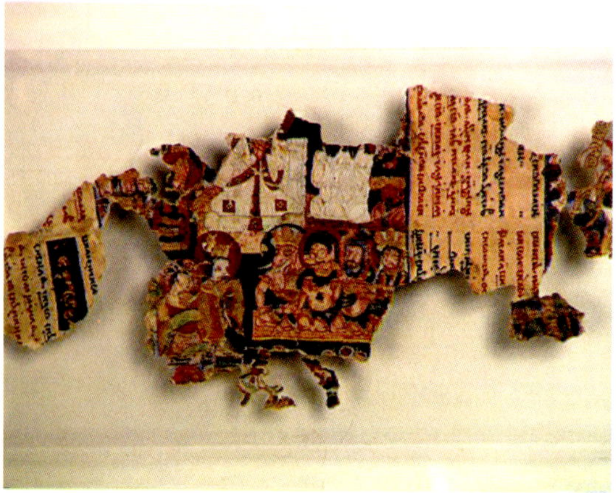

Prophet Mani

Mani was a second-century Persian who believed himself to be the saviour of mankind. Like the Zoroastrians, he believed that the world was based on two opposing principles: good and evil. Like Christ, Mani was crucified and his followers, the Manichaeans, fled eastward along the Silk Road. They continued to make converts and the faith survived for another 700 years. Le Coq's finds added enormously to our meagre knowledge of this extinct faith.

But he felt that an enormous treasure had been lost shortly before his arrival. A whole Manichaean library had been tossed into a river by a Muslim farmer fearful of blasphemy. Nonetheless, Le Coq found many important remains: a Byzantine-style mural from a small church belonging to the Nestorians, a Christian sect outlawed in the West in the year 432; Biblical texts in twenty-four different scripts; and a life-size statue of a headless Buddha. And finally, in an ancient cellar, the corpses of wounded Buddhists monks – evidence that they too had paid heavily for their beliefs.

One of the fresco paintings inside the Bezeklik Caves

Despite the riches which Le Coq had already uncovered, one of his biggest hauls was yet to come. Tucked away in the Flaming Mountains north of Karakhoja is the remote monastery of Bezeklik. It was the hidden centre of Buddhist worship for over a thousand years. The road follows a steep gauge carved by the Murtok river. Stone ramparts make natural cathedrals in the rock face. It is a perfect site for a religious community seeking refuge from the violent clash of cultures in this cauldron of Asia.

Bezeklik Caves

Bezeklik means 'Place where there are Paintings'. Over a hundred temples have been hewn out of the rock. There are sixty-seven cave temples cut out of the rock face, each with a spectacular mountain view. Most of the temples are arranged along a narrow terrace halfway up the rock. Originally, a path led to the top of the cliff and a ladder to the monastery below.

Encased in heaps of sand, Le Coq found a whole gallery of ancient murals in perfect condition. They dated from the fourth to the fourteenth century and encapsulated

Umberto Scapagnini at Bezeklik Caves

Michael Haggiag at Bezeklik Caves

Bezeklik Caves

the history of paintings in Central Asia. Le Coq recounts, 'I saw on the walls to my right and left splendid paintings in colours as fresh as if the artist had only just finished them ... By dint of long and arduous work, we succeeded in cutting away all these pictures ... This is one of the few temples whose sum total of paintings have been brought safely to Berlin.' (*Foreign Devils on the Silk Road: The Search for Lost Cities and Treasures of Chinese Central Asia*)

But they were not nearly as safe as Le Coq imagined. During World War II, allied bombs flattened the Ethnological Museum of Berlin. Many paintings and artifacts were saved but all the bigger murals that could not be moved were destroyed. Little remains to be seen of the great desert art gallery except the monastery itself, and the beauty of its natural setting. Today, the Chinese regard Albert von Le Coq simply as a thief, one of the many 'foreign devils' who stripped China of her heritage at a time when she was weak.

But in 1905, Le Coq could still feel he had secured his place in history as one of the world's great archaeologists. It was already the middle of summer and the heat in Turpan was becoming unbearable. Le Coq and his assistant Barthus decided to de-camp to Hami, 200 miles to the east across the Gobi desert. There they were lavishly entertained by the last Hami king, who despite being a Muslim, liked to drink French champagne. Within a year of Le Coq's death, the Chinese would reassert control over the region.

The tomb complex of the Hami kings, which includes an abandoned mosque, remains the city's most impressive monument. The mausoleums with their tiled domes and their cool verandas and their beautiful Chinese eaves, look like royal palaces, reminders of a gracious era.

Film show at Hami

Today Hami has a population of three lakhs. There are many different nationalities including Uighur, Kazakh, Hui and Mongol. But the majorities are Han Chinese. In summer, the city starts to come alive in the late afternoon, as the sun goes down. We find vendors in the Central Square preparing for the night bazaar. And the picture palace which tonight is showing a free

Scenes from Hami

Scenes from Hami (continued)

movie in the open air. Billiards is a favourite pastime in China and no night bazaar is without a good number of billiard tables. Uighur kebabs are the preferred fast food, but the Chinese serve their own cuisine as well.

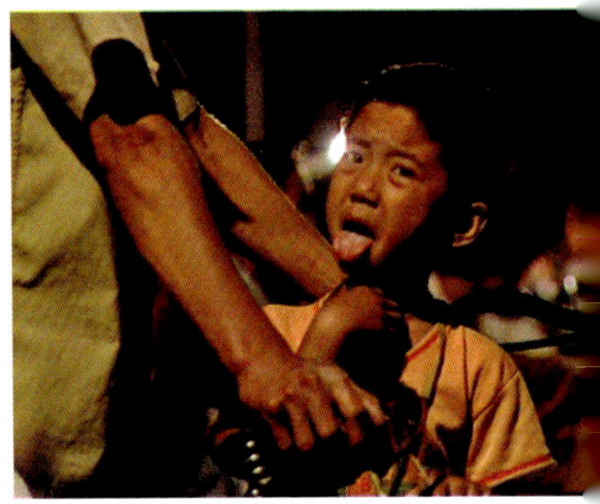

Faces at the Hami market

It is our 40th day on the road. We are heading towards Dunhuang, where the two arms of the Silk Road meet again at the tip of the desert. It is about 250 miles away and we plan to be there by nightfall. On horseback, it would have taken Le Coq seventeen days. Lacking the time, he headed back to Kashgar, and missed out on the greatest prize of all, the Dunhuang library from which Aurel Stein removed more than 10,000 manuscripts and wall hangings.

We reach Xingxingxia by lunch time. At the turn of the century, this barren ravine was the Chinese border with Turkestan. Soldiers manned the check-points and travellers were often delayed for days if they got through at all. Now it is simply a place to take our mid-day meal. We feed in whatever café we come to, so our guide, Liang Limin, tries to make sure we get here on time. Arrivals and departures are calculated to the minute and we are often chided for our lack of discipline. As always, the food is made to order. It hardly varies. We know the dishes now and are getting used to eating with chopsticks.

The time has taken on a new dimension. For a thousand years, Chinese travellers leaving Dunhuang for the west stopped at the Cave of the Thousand Buddhas to pray. They commissioned wall paintings in the cave temples as an offering for their safe return. Because of the dry climate, there are nearly 500 grottoes in good condition with over 45,000 murals and 2,000 painted statues. It is the richest collection of Buddhist art and literature in the world. Because of its remoteness, few westerners knew anything about the Mogao Caves until the early part of this century. Even today it is the least known of China's wonders.

The ruins of a Han dynasty Chinese watchtower made of rammed earth at Dunhuang

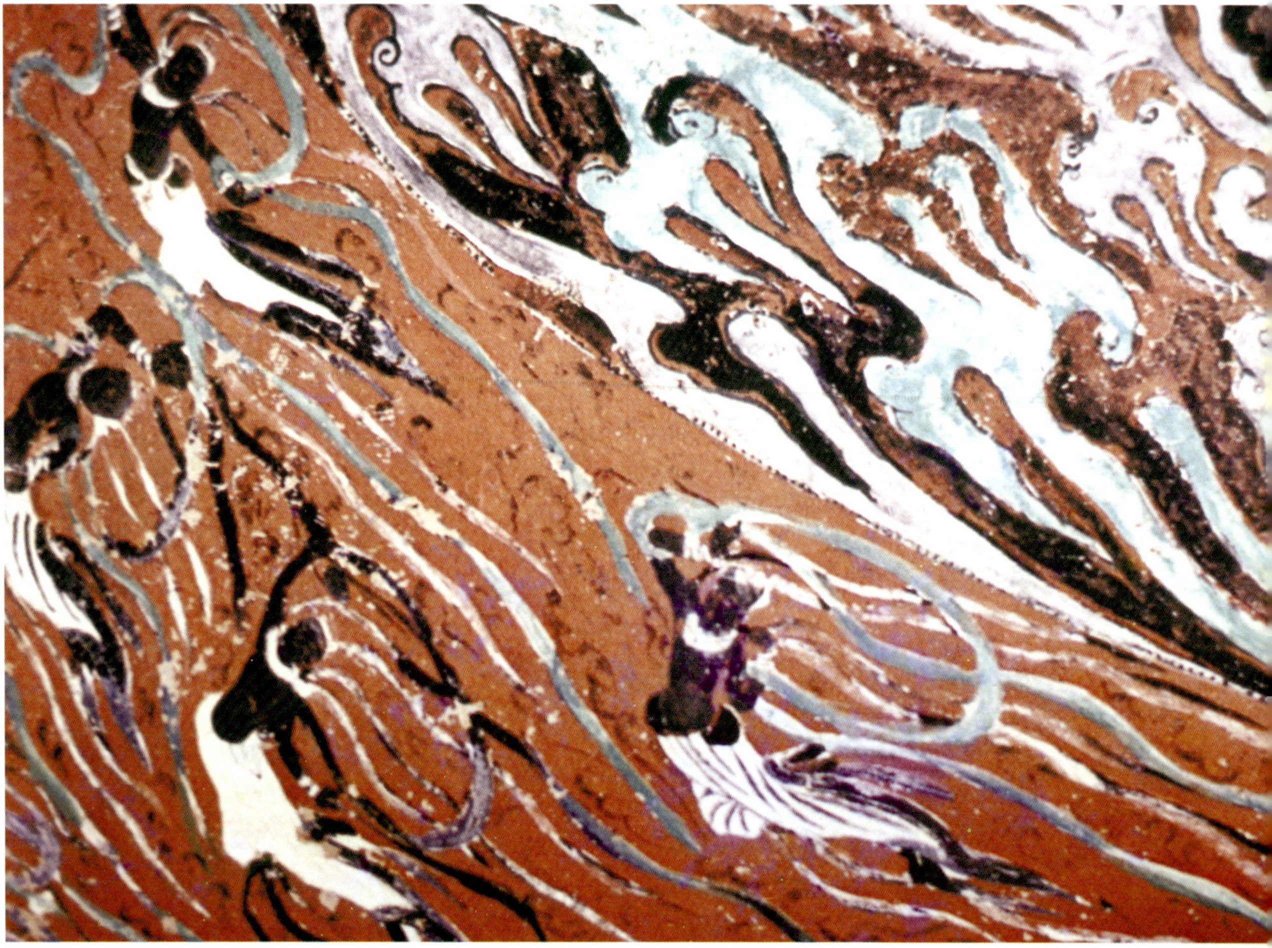

A mural within the Mogao Caves

A mural within the Mogao Caves (continued)

A mural within the Mogao Caves (continued)

A mural within the Mogao Caves (continued)

Photographs of Mogao Caves at Dunhuang taken by Aurel Stein

Aurel Stein first visited the Mogao Caves at the dawn of the twentieth century after hearing that a pile of manuscripts had been discovered behind a sealed wall in one of the temples. The man credited with the discovery was an eccentric called Wang. Wang came to the conclusion that he had been entrusted with the noble task of restoring the caves with his own statues and paintings. He needed funds for his monumental folly and to this end he thought of selling a portion of the 50,000 manuscripts he had found. Stein's reverence and passion for the Chinese pilgrim Xuanzang saved the day, for Wang regarded Xuanzang as his patron saint.

Michael has been following the trail of Xuanzang since our journey began, and is eager to see Cave 17. Michael explained to us, 'This is where the self-appointed abbot Wang handed Stein over 7,500 painted scrolls and manuscripts for a pittance, a mere sum of 120 pounds. The collection now finds pride of place in the British Library in London. Conservationists have to clean and arrange each item for scholars wishing to examine them. The manuscripts have been written in various languages long extinct. Dating from the first to the tenth century CE, they cover science, history, arts and economics as well as religion.'

~

A few months after the expedition we visited the British Museum to shoot the treasures of the Mogao Caves. The conversation between Michael and the curator in London …

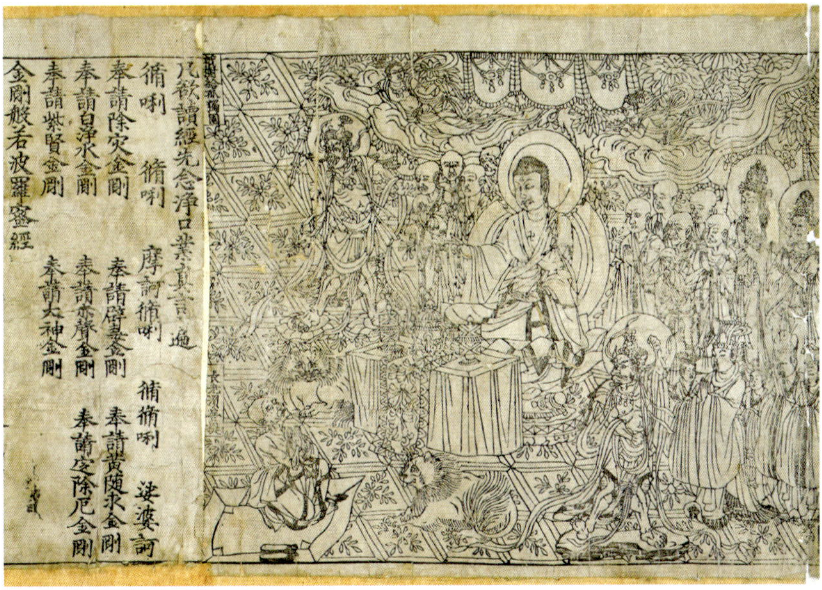

Above: Michael with the curator at British Museum; Below: Close-up of the Diamond Sutra

Michael: This is the oldest printed book in the world … the rarest of rare manuscript – the Diamond Sutra. One of British Museum's treasured possessions.

Curator: Yes, Stein found it, mixed up with thousands of other sutras in the Cave of the Thousand Buddhas in Dunhuang.

Michael: And is this the famous frontispiece?

Curator: Yes, it tells the story of the Diamond Sutra … that the Buddha here is preaching. He is answering questions posed by his funny little old disciple here, Subhūti ... sitting on a meditation mat with his shoes placed neatly beside him ... then you have Buddhist lines ... the Guardians of the faith ... and then a whole crowd of Bhikṣus and Bodhisattvas and the Chinese emperor all listening to the exposition of the sutra.

Michael: Amazing! What does this say here?

Curator: An instruction to the reader ... only allowed to be read by the faithful ... In order to read the sutra one must first possess a clean mouth. Only then the true words will spread all over the world.

Michael: In terms of the evolution of a book, how many years shall we have to wait before the emergence of the Gutenberg Bible?

Curator: Well, at least 500 years. This book was printed using wood block printing, a technique initiated by the Chinese. So this means that the Gutenberg Bible is way behind. However, by the time the Gutenberg Bible was being printed, the Chinese had also started using the book format that we are familiar with today.

Michael: This looks like calligraphy.

Curator: This is a result of first writing out the text in calligraphy. Next the Chinese printed the inscribed text using a wooden block. After that the paper would be pasted face down on a wooden block and the characters etched, so it is much closer.

The entrance to the Mogao Caves at Dunhuang

Another view of the Mogao Caves at Dunhuang

Michael: This is a long book.

Curator: The right end of the book is of great interest and importance because the date is inscribed here. It is 868 AD. The colophon says that it is made for universal free distribution by Wang Jie on behalf of his two parents on the 15th of the 4th moon of the 9th year of Xiantong. Wang Jie funded the printing of multiple copies of the book. He distributed the proceeds from the book to all the temples of China so that his deceased parents would gain heavenly union.

Unlike the rest of the Buddhist sites dotting the Silk Road, the Dunhuang caves were never completely abandoned because the natives considered it a sacred site. Excavations were thus out of the question, but Aurel Stein studied them carefully nonetheless. Stein writes,

In their freely drawn landscape backgrounds, their Chinese architecture, the bold movement and realism of their figures, a distinctly Chinese style prevailed. It was the same with the graceful and often fantastic freedom of the cloud scrolls, floral tracery, and other decorative motifs. But all the principal divine figures bore the unmistakable impress of Indian models transmitted through Central Asian Buddhism. Tradition preserved for these Buddhas, Bodhisattvas and their saintly attendants, the type of face, pose and drapery originally developed by Greco-Buddhist art. (*On Ancient Central Asian Tracks*)

The movie set encountered by the author in the middle of the desert

A Ming dynasty fortress stands against the backdrop of the Mingsha sand dunes. It is perfectly preserved, right down to the banners on its ramparts. But this is not due to the dry climate. In fact, it is an abandoned movie set. Fantasy takes hold of the dullest imagination in the desert, making one see and hear things that should not be there. Hari Ahluwalia imagines he is travelling along the Silk Road in a caravan all the way from Samarkand to Mount Everest. Whose dream was this fortress, I wonder? Is it true to history? But then it doesn't have to be true as long as it's convincing. And a movie set is never convincing until it has a story and characters to give it life: one I like concerns Marco Polo's fabled city of Etzina.

In 1908, the Russians made their first and only major discovery in Central Asia. At a remote spot in the Gobi desert, they were astonished to see rising from the desert a huge fortress city. The Russian explorers entered by the western gate that defined a large quadrangle with the scattered ruins of many buildings. The natives of a nearby oasis told them how the town came to be destroyed in the fourteenth century.

The last ruler was called Kara Tsian Tsiun. He thought his armies were invincible and dreamed of seizing the throne of China. But the emperor sent a large force against him and after several battles, laid siege to the rebel capital. The emperor's army was unable to take the walled city by direct assault, but managed to divert its water supply. The defenders dug a deep well, but finding no water, decided on one last battle. Kara Tsian Tsiun prepared himself for the inevitable. First he lowered his treasury, comprising eighty carts of gold, into the well. Next, he killed his two wives, his son and his daughter to keep them from falling into enemy hands. Finally, he made a breach through one of the walls and charged out to meet his fate. His once invincible army was smashed and he himself killed in battle. The emperor razed the city in search of the missing gold but never found it. Legend has it that Kara Tsian Tsiun cast a spell over the spot before charging to his death. The Russians failed as well to find the gold and so it remains hidden to this day. The afternoon sun casts a golden light over the dunes. They are changing shape by the hour, by the day, by the century, covering the past yet somehow preserving it too ... as an ancestral memory, to haunt the dreams of each successive generation.

Road to Tibet

ON THE ROOF OF THE WORLD

It is the 46th day of our journey. We pitched camp at Qaidam Pendi, a cold desert 9,000 ft above sea level. Lhasa, also known as the Forbidden City, is 1,300 miles away.

Rawat became part of our expedition in order to follow the trail of his grandfather Kishen Singh and his great uncle Naim Singh who surveyed Tibet clandestinely for the British. In 1865, accounts of Russian infiltration of Tibet alarmed the British for Tibet was a blank space on the maps of the British empire. Sending officers to spy for them didn't help since the British secret agents would always be caught. Things started changing after Captain Montgomery, Chief Surveyor of India, trained native school teachers as surveyors. They surveyed the entire Tibetan plateau on foot by themselves, and came up with impressively accurate maps. At present we are waiting at the foot of the three-mile-

Qaidam Pendi camp

high plateau, catching our breath and acclimatizing ourselves before retracing the steps of Kishen Singh, a Buddhist pilgrim in disguise.

Images of Old Tibet

This final leg of our journey into Tibet has been long awaited. Tibet means 'distant unknown land' in Turkic. The name itself is a siren song for exploration – venturing into the unknown. Since the closing of the last century Tibet has witnessed a succession of remarkable travellers trying to breach its borders in search of the forbidden city of Lhasa. However, almost all of them failed. The ever-expanding Russian empire to the north and the British Raj in India ensured that Tibet closed ranks and refused entry to all westerners. The few exceptions were a small diplomatic presence maintained by the Chinese, merchants from northern India, and pilgrims from the neighbouring Buddhist countries of Nepal, Bhutan and Mongolia.

The road here is under military control and it is a security-sensitive area with few foreign travellers. Sven Hedin called Tibet the most stupendous upheaval to be found on the face of the planet. I can well imagine why after climbing up the mountain roads the entire day. Our jeep approaches the Tangula Pass on the Kunlun Shan mountains at a height of 15,000 ft. This is one of the highest roads in the world. Our first designated halt is just below a string of mountain peaks each one at least 18,000 ft high. Yet from this height, they seem strangely dwarfish. The Tibetan plateau spreads out on all sides like a vast table-land, punctuated by snow-capped oriental chimneys.

Even after 400 miles of non-stop driving none of us can build up an appetite. We have started experiencing the ill effects of oxygen depravation – light-headedness, headache, queasiness and a feeling of heaviness weighing down on the chest and limbs. We become the object of scrutiny for the local people outside the café. This is a rare sight

Chortens

for them. I wonder what they think of us huddling together in this small room speaking all at once in many different alien tongues.

At some point after the Tangula Pass we left behind the boundary of Old Tibet. In the absence of signboards it is impossible to fathom where the boundary of the ancient kingdom once began. Our trip is turning out to be rather challenging even on this modern road. One has to keep in mind that the Tibetan plateau is a huge landmass, roughly equivalent to Europe – and at this height it is akin to a continent floating in the sky.

Ann Taylor (left) and Susie Reinhardt (right)

Sven Hedin among Tibetans

Among the early travellers who risked life and limb in their quest for Lhasa, were some extraordinary women with fantastic tales. Ann Taylor was a fearless Christian missionary, Susie Reinhardt had to bury her baby in the snow, and Alexandra David-Néel was the first European woman to become a Tibetan Lama. She is known for her writings on Tibet. Unfortunately her descriptions of paranormal occurences were so far-fetched that they were not taken seriously by many. Alexandra David-Néel's contribution lies in her accurate sketches of everyday life in Tibet at a time when the world knew next to nothing about Tibetan habits and customs.

Some thirty years prior to this, in 1902 the Swedish explorer Sven Hedin was bold enough to attempt entering Lhasa. Disguised as a Mongolian pilgrim on horseback he was accompanied by two Indian surveyors, specially recruited for this mission. Before long they were politely sent away by an emissary of the Dalai Lama and Lhasa continued to remain out of bounds. Hedin would of course later retrace his steps and successfully map Tibet's diverse physical features. His comprehensive geological report is among the most exhaustive surveys ever made. However, two more years passed before Lhasa allowed outsiders entry.

Alexandra David-Néel

Yaks in Tibetan landscape

A meadow full of yaks is the first sign of human settlement as we go into the heart of Tibet. These shaggy-haired cattle with humped shoulders are indigenous to the Himalayan region and are the only 'beasts of burden' that can withstand this altitude. Tibet and China are closely bound by their past. Way back in the seventh century, the Tibetan kingdom had annexed much of western China including its imperial capital Shangang. However, China has gained the upper hand and is the dominant power in the region.

When the Maoist soldiers marched into Tibet in 1950, the Chinese called the event 'peaceful liberation'. They maintained in their heads that they had freed Tibet from isolation and feudalism. The military built a road – an architectural marvel – that linked Tibet with the mainland and thus ensured a smooth supply line for the Chinese troops. The Chinese used this road to take over all of Tibet. By 1970 the scenario had changed with the native economy collapsing. Chinese supplies, now urgently required, came down this road.

Tibet has within its massive landmass, uniquely placed, a treasure trove of knowledge about the earth's evolution and weather patterns. The abundance of minerals and natural resources here must be an exciting proposition for a vast and fast growing industrial nation. While China may have been eager to exploit Tibet's natural resources, it could not have been euphoric about the millions of new dependents.

We have been travelling across Tibet for days now without sighting a single town. After the Chinese divided Tibet into many parts the eastern provinces of Kham and Amdo were no longer part of Tibet. This left the interiors of Tibet with about two million people, only a third of its population once.

Nachu is a Tibetan marketplace only 200 miles from Lhasa. Interestingly it lies in close proximity to the modern border of inner Tibet. One can see Chinese retail stores, tractors, trucks and bicycles everywhere. After being rebuilt in 1950 by the Chinese, it mirrors the new reality of the last four decades.

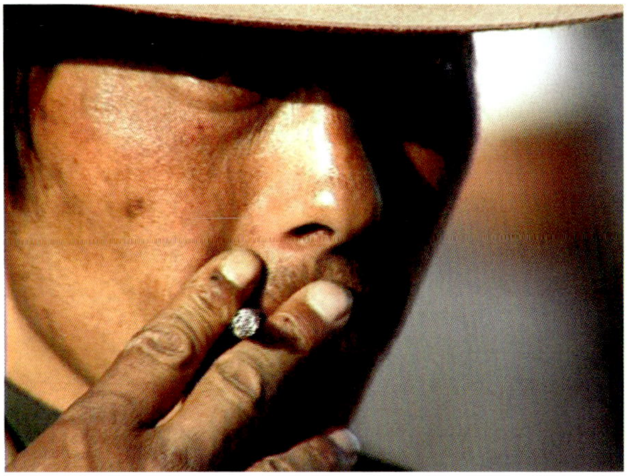

Tibetans with cowboy hats

Buddhist pilgrim making full-length prostrations

We feel straight out of a Western movie set in a frontier town in the American Old West. Grimy men in cowboy hats pitching posts for horses and yaks, and long-haired natives who look eerily similar to Native American Indians complete this picture. All this in spite of Chinese red flags fluttering overhead. To them we must appear equally alien and fantastic. Their silent eyes ask us: *What is our purpose here? Are we friends or foes? What new world does our presence foreshadow?*

It is an important day for Nachu. The local school board is celebrating forty years of communist education and the childrens' marching bands are waiting for the big parade to begin. Our arrival seems to give a special flavour to the occasion.

Like everywhere else, the old traditions live on longest in the countryside. We discover a Buddhist pilgrim making full-length prostrations every few feet. He is making a holy pilgrimage in the age-old manner of those who seek spiritual merit. The practice exists in India too, even among Hindus, but one rarely sees it today. *Is he going all the way to Lhasa, some two hundred miles away, or to a shrine nearby?*

Buddhism was introduced by Indian missionaries in the seventh century. Few places in the world have experienced the impact of religion as profoundly as Tibet. It conditioned the very structure of the society and affected every aspect of daily life.

On the way to Lhasa, we see our first caravan of yaks. I am delighted to see there are Chinese roads that have not yet eclipsed this traditional mode of transport. Clearly Tibet, like India, has many layers to its economy with the old ways of life persisting in parallel with the modern infrastructure.

A high mountain pass

Bejoy Anand with indigenous Tibetans

We have descended to a mere 12,000 ft above sea level. The mysterious city of Lhasa lies just over the next ridge. Damsum Valley is the ancient bread-basket of inner Tibet. After the Chinese took over, there were attempts to grow rice and wheat which failed because of the high altitudes. Now the fields are once again bursting with traditional rapeseed and barley. Summer is a time of renewed activity after the long winter months indoors. The snow melts into fast-flowing streams which irrigate the precious crops. Tibetans live close to nature and treat her with utmost respect. Prayer flags serve to propitiate her spirit and pacify her powers. When Buddhism arrived in Tibet, her former gods were transformed into protective deities, psychological counterparts to the dangerous forces of the natural world.

In addition to religious rites, there are the seasonal rituals of daily life. Washing and bathing are communal activities reserved almost exclusively for the warm months. Although impatient to reach Lhasa, we are directed to a carwash outside the city for a ritual ablution of our own. It is compulsory but cheap. There is a tradition in India that before entering a holy place, everything should be washed and purified. Could this be what's happening here?

Rising a thousand feet above the floor of the Lhasa river valley is the Potala Palace, home of the god-kings of Tibet. Perched on the top of an isolated crag in the centre of the city, it can be seen from miles around. For thirteen centuries, Tibet was ruled by a religious hierarchy of Lamas or priests headed by the Dalai Lama. This 1,000-roomed palace served as the twin seats of power – religious and political.

Tibet was a feudal kingdom until about the first few decades of this century. It had all the trappings of a monarchy and was ruled with pomp and ceremony. The first European travellers must have felt that they had walked into a realm of fantasy. The British ambassador Basil Gould recorded a home movie in 1936. Little did he know that he was recording for posterity the last scenes of an ancient way of life. This unique civilization faded into history a few years after his visit. Among other things, he had recorded the present Dalai Lama, then only a child, being led on horseback in a ceremonial parade. A couple of decades later the Tibetans would be dancing to a very different tune – Chairman Mao's communism.

We enter the inner sanctum of the Dalai Lama like over-awed pilgrims, eager to see what secrets lie within. It is eerily silent. We find floor upon floor of empty rooms and corridors. The Potala Palace is devoid of any sign of vandalism. We are informed that in the late 1960s China's premier, Zhou Enlai, was very particular about protecting the

Litho of Potala Palace

palace while the Red Guard was demolishing large chunks of China's heritage in the guise of cultural revolution. There hangs a desolate air about the place in spite of being well preserved. Stripped of its former power and position it has been reduced to a museum now.

The Potala was where all treaties were signed, religious ceremonies performed, and all important decisions pertaining to the country taken. The palace observed between ten and twelve festivals a year. The great prayer, observed for three weeks beginning with the New Year, attracted large crowds every year, pushing up Lhasa's small population manifold. They prayed for the well being of the humankind and all of the animal kingdom with a special blessing for the people of Tibet.

We are on the quiet roof of the empty palace. I hear a faint song rising from the terrace below me and the rhythmic tapping of sticks. The Tibetans are celebrating the Dalai Lama's birthday. The distant sound of firecrackers and car horns can be heard. By a strange coincidence, we are in the Potala Palace on the anniversary of the god-king's birth.

Interiors of Potala Palace

Potala Palace

Like any other cosmopolitan city the modern and the traditional coexist in Lhasa. There are pilgrims spinning metal prayer wheels at the Potala and chanting the ancient Buddhist invocation: *'Om Manipadme Hum'* (Hail Jewel in the Lotus). Across the congested street is a Chinese restaurant whose façade could be straight out of a fashion magazine.

Watching the beggar children entertain Hari beside the prayer drums of the Potala, it occurs to me that I have yet to see any trace of the pious gloominess I often associate with religion. Here is a fine example of the secular and the sacred living in perfect harmony. The prayer wheels lining the temple walls are never idle. With every turn of the wheel, a prayer rises up for mankind's well being. Meanwhile the children have great fun spinning the prayer wheels.

Jokhang, Tibet's oldest temple, attracts throngs of pilgrims from all over Tibet. It is situated in Barkhor, known as the old quarter of Lhasa, and is both a holy shrine and a bustling marketplace. Pilgrims from far and near circumambulate the temple at all hours of the day and night. Killing two birds with one stone, they have a good look at the shops and their wares while chanting their prayers. There are devout pilgrims who go the extra mile and offer full prostration, where the length of their bodies act as a measure of their progress while circling the temple clockwise. All of it add up as acts of faith and help in cleansing past sins. The concept of Karma is central to Buddhism. All human acts, including prayers, have consequences be it in this life or the next. Prayers are powerful and when offered by a devout pilgrim can set aside the ill effects of past actions leading to a wiser understanding of the present.

Jokhang Temple was originally built by the young Tibetan king Songtsen Gampo in the seventh century to house and worship the Buddhist statues brought by his Chinese and Nepalese wives. The king was persuaded by his two princesses to convert from the Bon faith to Buddhism. Thus began the astounding metamorphosis of a fierce warrior tribe into one of the gentlest and peace-loving race of all.

There is a monastic cloister in the inner courtyard where young monks are initiated in the art of spiritual sparring. What I first take to be a violent argument turns out to be no more than a good-natured contest of wits.

The monks had to face violence and torture when China occupied Tibet. Even Jokhang was not spared. The Chinese wanted to put an end to Lamaism which they perceived as an enemy of the Communist ideology. That struck the death knell for religion. Temples and monasteries were ransacked, demolished and closed down. Lamas and monks were forcibly de-frocked and reduced to lay men. This religious persecution continued

Jokhang Temple

The entrance to Jokhang Temple

Destruction of Ganden monastery

unabated from 1959 to 1978. Much of Tibet's ancient heritage was lost irrevocably.

When the Chinese realized that brute force has failed to wipe out Tibet's faith they went about unobstrusively reversing their stance. A more temperate wind started blowing in China once the Red Guards and the infamous Gang of Four fell out of favour. Monks could return to their monasteries and public worship was reinstated. May this gentle and peace-loving race never have to endure such torture and destruction again.

The West has come to Tibet which no longer lives in splendid isolation on the Roof of the World. Both cultures have something to offer each other. But I wonder what all this global chatter has to do with the deep stillness of Tibet's majestic mountains.

Sera, Drepung and Ganden are three monasteries in the vicinity of Lhasa that had significant political and religious power. Situated at the base of Tatipur hill on the northern fringe of Lhasa, Sera was famous for its niche army of soldier-monks, known as Dob-dobs, renowned for their athletic feats and occasional acts of rebellion.

When monasteries ruled Tibet more than one-fifth of the population consisted of celibate monks. A monk brought honour to his family and every family would send at least one son to be raised in a monastery. Boys can become monks at the tender age of seven. However, only the brightest among them grow up to be scholarly lamas.

Once populated by over 7,000 monks, today Sera's chapels and chanting halls have a desolate look. Occasionally a gilded statute or an ancient wall-hanging break through the gloom offering us a glimpse of past grandeur.

Marketplace near Jokhang Temple

Marketplace near Jokhang Temple (continued)

Drepung monastery

Drepung is Tibet' largest and most influential monastery. At the height of its glory, over 10,000 monks resided there. Drepung's lamas are tasked with the job of training each young Dalai Lama to take over as leader of the nation. The sense of desolation hangs like a thick blanket all around. We discover that around 400 monks and novices are currently residing in Drepung. One of the four heavenly kings stands guard at the entrance of a temple. A faded stencil of Chairman Mao recalls the terrifying days of the Red Guards. In this more tolerant time artistes are busy redecorating the old temples with modern murals that try to replicate the ancient wall-paintings done to the last detail.

In Buddhism the cycle of creation, destruction and recreation of the universe is an endless one. A freshly painted Buddha sits enshrined with Tibetan deities looking on from all sides. Among them is the multi-headed Shan Rezi, the Bodhisattva of compassion. The Dalai Lama is supposed to be his living incarnation. Perhaps we are witnessing the hopeful preparations for his return home.

The Ganden is the oldest and most sacred monastery of the Yellow Hats, the priestly sect of all Dalai Lamas. It is built on a beautiful crescent-shaped ridge. A stronghold of Tibetan resistance, it was taken by assault in 1959, the day the Chinese bombarded the hill with heavy artillery, and by the time its last monk surrendered, there was little left of Ganden except its charred foundations. But even here, the spirit of renewal is apparent. Local volunteers are rebuilding Ganden in their spare time and we learn that 200 monks have already taken up residence here.

Ganden monastery

The seventh Dalai Lama built a summer palace here in 1755 to avail himself of its curative waters. Norbulingka means 'Jewel Park'. And his successors later built their own houses in pavilions. The Dalai Lama's move from the Potala to Norbulingka in the spring was the occasion for a splendid annual procession. Lamas, nobles, musicians and soldiers all paraded on horseback, carrying huge banners while the God-king rode by in a closed palanquin. Today Norbulingka is called 'The People's Park' and, like the Potala, it is no more than a museum.

Buddhist priest at Norbulingka

I fall into conversation with a solitary gate-keeper in the courtyard of the present abbot's residence. I offer him a cigarette. As a gesture of reciprocation, he tells me a story. 'There used to be a lake that was periodically fed by a natural spring and would remain empty at other times. An embellished pair of pavilions

Norbulingka Palace

adorn a small island in the middle of this lake. The Chinese, unaware of the natural spring, poured concrete into the basin and filled it with water. However, the new water kept seeping away leaving the basin dry. The natural spring never came back.'

Soon after their invasion, the Chinese set about dismantling the old order in Tibet, eager to replace it with a newer Communist model. But one institution was preserved and even expanded – Tibetan medicine. In the hospital, Tibetan doctors provide effective and occasionally remarkable treatment for several hundred patients a day using a range of more than 2,000 naturally prepared medicines.

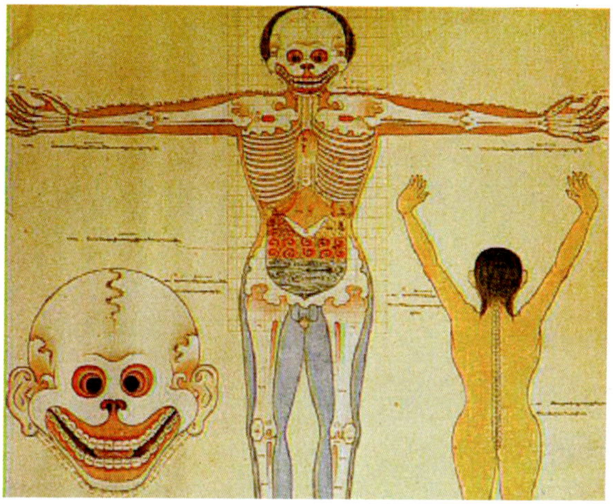

Page from Medical Sutra

Unknown until recently to the outside world, Tibetan medicine is a highly sophisticated branch in Buddhist knowledge dating back to ancient times. It was developed in the monasteries of northern India and first introduced into Tibet in the first century BCE. It has been further enriched by Chinese medicine and a vast pharmacopeia of remedies unique to the Himalaya. The oral traditions of Indian Ayurvedic medicine, many of which have been lost over the centuries, are still preserved in the pictures and scrolls found in Lhasa.

Tibetan medical theory evolved from various sources. Knowledge of anatomy came from the Chinese, and complex surgery was performed until it was banned by a Tibetan king in the ninth century. But the greatest influence of all was exerted by Tibet's native genius, Yuthok Gonpo. Tantric scrolls describe 84,000 illnesses in over 1,600 divisions. They include everything from anatomy, pathology and embryology to diagnosis and treatment. Yet throughout the text, the emphasis is placed on the well-being of the whole patient rather than on the particular disease. In Tibet, medicine and religion are closely related. The Buddha himself compared his teaching to the healing of the sick. If a man is shot by a poisoned arrow, said the Buddha, *he should not ask who shot it or why* but quickly remove the arrow so that the wound may start to heal.

Tibet has received her share of poisoned arrows and is busy removing them. *Is it too late for her wounds to heal?* Lhasa has suffered many intruders intent on exposing her

Tibetan medical centre in Lhasa

mysteries. The early travellers, the British, the Chinese, and now us. Old Tibet is gone and no country can turn back the clock and few would wish to. The faith and spirit of the people remain a mystery and this traveller for one is content to leave it so.

Old woman with a prayer wheel

Children in this country are considered special since any one of them may be an old and pious Lama reincarnated

Children of Tibet

Little monk with movie camera

They say he is an 'incarnated Lama' and heir prince of a Himalayan throne, but I doubt his reality. Probably he will vanish like a mirage, with his caparisoned little steed and his party of followers, dressed in all the colours of the rainbow. He is a part of the enchantment in which I have lived these last fifteen years. This new episode is of the stuff that dreams are made of. In a few minutes, I shall wake up in a real bed, in some country not haunted by genii nor by 'incarcerated Lamas' wrapped in shimmering silk. A country where men wear ugly dark coats and the horses do not carry silver inlaid saddles on yellow-yellow cloths.

The sound of the kettledrum makes me start, two hautboys intone a melancholy minor tune. The youthful genie straddles his diminutive courser, knights and squires jump into their saddles.

'I shall expect you', the lama-prince says, smiling graciously at me. I hear myself, as if I were listening to some other person, promising him that I will start the next day for his capital, and the little troop, headed by the musicians, disappears.

As the last murmurs of the plaintive melody die away in the distance, the enchantment that has held me spellbound dissipates.

– Alexandra David-Néel

Magic and Mystery in Tibet

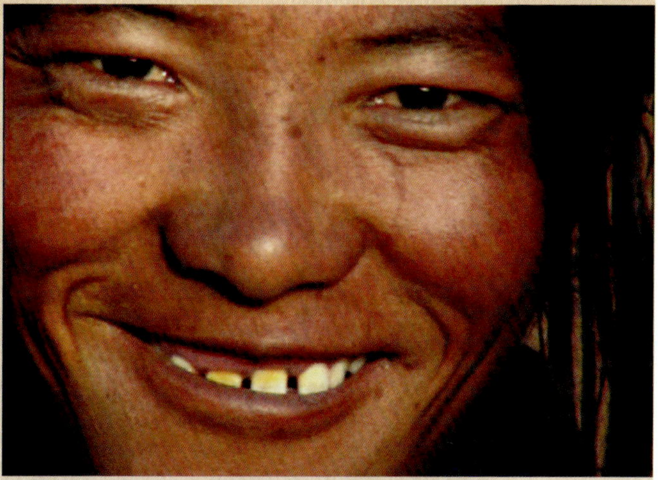

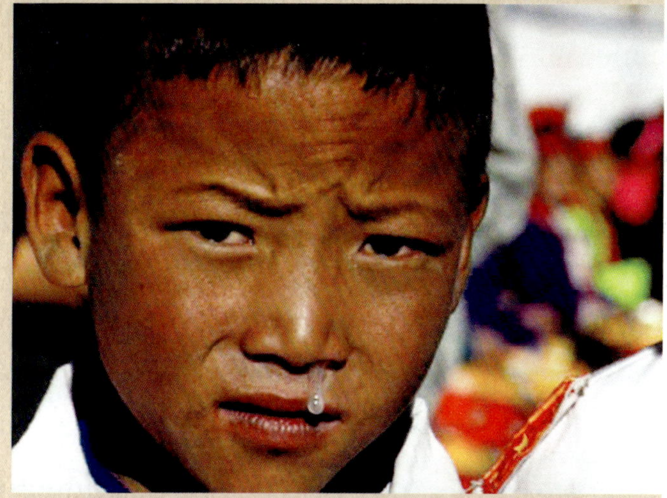

A Typical Tibetan house

A horse cart in Tibet

HIGHER THAN EVEREST

We leave Lhasa behind today as we set off for the last leg of our expedition. We shall have to go across the heart of old Tibet on a journey that will take us into the Himalayas. Lhasa Bridge is covered in prayer flags to celebrate the birthday of the absent Dalai Lama.

We have gathered here to say goodbye to Hari, the leader of our expedition. It is a sad moment. Hari travelled with us into Lhasa to join us on the last leg of our journey to Everest. But the sudden change of altitude has affected him badly and he will not be able to continue. After a few words of advice, he falls silent, overcome by emotion. Hari climbed Everest in 1965 but he has had to give up his dream of seeing the mountain again.

Heading west we come across a brightly coloured rock carving of the Buddha. It reminds me of the Buddhist principle about all things being in a state of flux. This concept is reinforced as it were by the spate of quick changes in atmospheric condition that we experience. The thin mountain air can neither block nor trap the sun's warmth. Consequently the mercury plummets whenever clouds appear. A scorching sandstorm without warning turns into a severe snowstorm which gives way to an abrupt downpour. It is said that in Tibet all four seasons can be encountered in one day.

The author shooting on location

Now that the sky has cleared we feel warm again. We

Avalokiteśvara

have been following the Lhasa river as it turned into the roaring Yarlung Tsangpo, Tibet's longest river. It is the highest major river in the world and aptly titled Tsangpo, meaning the mighty one. It plunges down 11,000 ft to enter India where it is known as the great Brahmaputra, son of Brahma, the Creator. But after merging with the Ganges to form the vast delta which flows into the Bay of Bengal, it takes the feminine name of Yamuna, Goddess of fertility and rebirth.

From left to right: Vignettes from the planting festival on the way to Shigatse

As we emerge from the gorge, we chance upon a planting festival. The season for growing crops is brief and often uncertain. So it is natural for farmers to pray for a good harvest. The festival is an ancient fertility ritual accompanied by music, singing and dancing. This old man waving his sword may be performing a rain dance or simply amusing the children. But the horsemen leaning over to touch the ground are clearly planting the first symbolic seeds of the season.

Today is the 7th of July. A routine break in our journey turns into an impromptu celebration when someone informs us that we have covered 10,000 kilometres since we began the expedition. We have covered Samarkand in Central Asia to Shigatse in Central Tibet in a little over ten weeks. Shigatse is Tibet's second largest city. It is situated in a wide picturesque valley close to the confluence of the Yarlung Tsangpo and Nianchu rivers.

Tashilhunpo is one of the important monasteries of the Yellow Hat sect, situated at the foot of Mount Drolmari, towards the western edge of Shigatse. Tashilhunpo is a city within a city. It is surrounded by a modern-day Chinese suburb. As we approach we can hear voices singing together. Expecting chanting monks we are taken aback at the sight before us. There are men and women working at a building site. Could this be a remnant of servitude from Tibet's medieval past? Or is it an outcome of fervent faith?

Shigatse town and monastery

Shigatse monastery

Scenes from Tashilhunpo

The Panchen Lama, the second-highest ranking spiritual leader of Tibet, resides at the Tashilhunpo. Panchen means 'great scholar'. The fifth Dalai Lama requested his teacher to accept this title when he accorded him Divine Status equal to his own. The fifth Dalai Lama also began the tradition of searching for the Panchen Lama's next incarnation after his death. The selection process of a Panchen Lama is thus similar to that of the Dalai Lama. The seventeenth century onwards, the Panchen and Dalai Lamas have been involved in each other's initiation, the elder mentoring the younger. The relationship has had its share of strife and discord. Foreign powers have time and again attempted entry into Tibet by turning one leader against the other.

Tashilhunpo, like the Potala Palace, attracts hordes of tourists. The courtyard of the Kelsang Temple is packed with camera-toting Chinese tourists. Tashilhunpo was once the administrative hub of Western Tibet. Fifty years ago 4,000 monks in four tantric colleges, each headed by its own abbot, comprised the nerve-centre of this region. There are over 600 monks including many young novices. Its quiet streets feel peaceful rather than desolate. It could be that Tashilhunpo's primary function still remains relevant.

Tashilhunpo was once the administrative hub of Western Tibet

Large numbers of Tibetan pilgrims reinforce this belief as they roll the prayer wheels of Tashilhunpo every day and circumambulate the monastery.

I can feel travel fatigue setting in and the disorienting altitude of Tibet is not helping either. For a moment though I get caught up in the rituals and I feel free of all worries just like the pilgrims I have been observing. For a millennium, Tibet was ruled by its faith; men for whom the world was a mirage constructed in the mind. I see prayer flags fluttering in the wind. I wonder what is really moving – the flags or the wind? Who can say? Is it not the mind that moves?

Shalu monastery lies fourteen miles south of Shigatse. It is a small monastery renowned for imparting psychic skills and training long-distance runners called 'Lungompas'. It is said that Lungompas acted as couriers navigating Tibet's vast expanses with superhuman leaps in a trance-like state. This was before the British inducted their postal and telegraphic services at the dawn of the new century.

The lamas of Shalu were also known for the practice of *Tummo* – ability to increase their body temperatures to fight the cold. This extraordinary feat was first reported by

Gyantse

The Zong or the fortress of Gyantse

the French Buddhist scholar Alexandra David-Néel in her book *Magic and Mystery in Tibet* (1971). She claimed that years of steadfast meditation helped her to master the technique. In her book she stressses that she did not meditate in order to become a miracle worker. She wants to highlight the subjective nature of all earthly phenomena and attain enlightenment.

Gyantse lies on the old caravan route from India and Nepal. Located at the head of the Nianchu Valley, it was the hub of trading for centuries. While acting as a gateway to the world outside, Gyantse was also situated at the forefront of any invasion from the south. Gyantse Zong or Gyantse fortress weathered attacks from India, Ladakh and Nepal but finally caved in to the British in 1904.

The British Viceroy Lord Curzon had long feared that Russia and Tibet had entered into a secret pact which threatened British India. Consequently he ordered a diplomatic mission to Tibet to investigate and confirm his worst fears. Col. Francis Younghusband, an imperial adventurer, was in charge of the mission. Younghusband decided to turn his expedition into a proper military invasion. The British easily overpowered the Tibetans at Yangtse. The antiquated muzzle-loaded muskets and spells cast by the Tibetans could not counter the destructive capacity of the superior British weapons. Seven hundred Tibetans were butchered in four days. The battle lost, the rest retreated in shock and disbelief.

Francis Younghusband

Younghusband entered Lhasa in August 1904 preceded by a marching band. The people of Lhasa waved, shouted and clapped in a desperate bid to stop the entry of the evil spirit. But Younghusband mistook that for a warm welcome and was most delighted. He discovered that the Dalai Lama had fled to Mongolia. Next he used force and coercion to make the unfortunate Tibetans accept a friendship treaty, known subsequently as the Treaty of Lhasa. Before leaving he ensured that a telegraph line and a trade mission in Gyantse were in place.

While the Tibetans' faith in their protective deities suffered a crushing blow, the expedition only added to Younghusband's mistaken notions of colonial conquest. Col. Francis Younghusband turned to spirituality in later life and went on to establish the World Congress of Faiths.

A thousand monks used to reside at the ancient Pelkor Chode monastery in Gyantse at one time. At present there are seventeen monks residing here, spending most of their time meditating and praying. The workers engaged in repairwork on the roof of the chanting hall seem to be echoing the chants of the monks below. The proximity between religion and everyday life in Tibet strikes me once more. Perhaps this right here explains the concept of the internal and external world's oneness in Buddhism. The prayers chanted inside the hall merge seemlessly with the restoration work without. Even a lay man in Tibet sees his life as a spiritual journey which culminates in liberation from worldly worries. The mountain is the metaphor for this journey. Every individual traverses his own path and makes the climb in his own time from the lowly rungs of ignorance to the pinnacle of wisdom. This journey may be stretched across many lives but the starting point happens to be the present time, from wherever one may be on the mountain.

Above: Old archival paintings of Younghusband's expedition to Tibet in 1904

The Storming of Gyantse Jong

Above: Route of Younghusband's mission to Tibet

Gyantse, which had been our goal for so many months, and with which we were to be but too well acquainted before we had finished, has two principal features the Jong and the monastery, called Palkhor Choide. The Jong is a really imposing structure built of strong, solid masonry, and rising in tiers of walls up a rocky eminence springing abruptly out of the plain to a height of 400 or 500 feet. It has a most commanding and dominant look. And the monastery immediately adjoining it at the base of the hill is also impressive from the height and solidity of the walls with which it is surrounded ...

On June 26 we reached Gyantse, after encountering considerable opposition at the village and monastery of Niani, which was held by 800 Tibetans. The fight lasted from 10 a.m. till 2 p.m., Colonel Brander from Gyantse assisting by occupying the hills above the village. Major Lye, 23rd Pioneers, was here severely wounded in the hand and slightly in the head. On its arrival our force was ineffectually bombarded from the Jong.

General Macdonald had now to break up the Tibetan force investing Gyantse. On the 28th he attacked a strong position on a ridge on which were the Tse-chen monastery and several fortified towers and sangars. The process of clearing the villages in the plain below lasted most of the day. At 5, the position itself was stormed by the 8th Gurkhas and the 40th Pathans, supported by the mountain battery. The fight was severe, for the hillside was very steep. Captain Craster, 46th Pathans, was killed whilst gallantly leading his company, and Captains Bliss and Humphreys slightly wounded. The capture of this position much disheartened the Tibetans; communications between Gyantse Jong and Shigatse were cut off, and the Jong was now surrounded on three sides.

Hearing that the big Lama from Lhasa, known as the Ta Lama, was at Shigatse, and that the Councillor was at Nagartse, on the road to Lhasa, I made a Lama in our employ write to these two on June 28, saying that the Tongsa Penlop had told me that they wished to come here to settle matters, but were afraid. I promised them, if they had proper credentials to effect a settlement, to guarantee their safety and treat them with respect; but I said they must come at once, for we were about to start for Lhasa. These letters I sent by the hands of prisoners. One of these messengers was seized by the Tibetans and brought to the Jong, where a council was held to consider its contents, as a result of which, on the following morning, a messenger with a flag of truce of enormous dimensions was sent to the Mission post. The whole garrison crowded to the walls to see his arrival, for this was the first indication of peace. He said the Tibetan leaders desired an armistice till the Ta Lama, who was at Penam, halfway to Shigatse, and who could be at Gyantse on the following day, could arrive to negotiate with me. The messenger said that he and the

Councillor coming from Nagartse had powers from the Dalai Lama. After consultation with General Macdonald, I replied to the Tibetans that I would grant the armistice they asked for till sunset of June 30, to enable the Ta Lama to reach Gyantse; but that as I was attacked on May 5 without warning, though I had informed the Tibetan Government that I was ready to negotiate there, and as Tibetan armed forces had occupied the Jong and fired into my camp ever since General Macdonald, who was responsible for the safety of the Mission, demanded that they should evacuate the Jong and withdraw all armed force beyond Karo-la, Yang-la, and Dongtse. A reasonable time for this would be given.

– Francis Younghusband

Extract from *India and Tibet* (1910) by Francis Younghusband

The multi-tiered Kumbum Temple is a visual treat and the architectural high point for me in Tibet. It was constructed by Newari artists from Nepal in the fifteenth century. The pagoda boasts twenty chapels, each having a protective deity and adorned with beautiful murals. Pilgrims make their way to all the chapels, their act of ascending

A close-up of Kumbum Temple's multi-tiered pagoda

the stupa being a symbolic journey toward salvation. Restoration work on the dome is in full swing and the scaffolding covers much of the façade. But I finally manage to spot the fabled 'all-seeing' benign eyes of wisdom. Indians place these eyes on vehicles and at places of worship to avert accidents and ward off ill omens.

A panoramic view of Kumbum Temple

Geologically the Himalayas came up just the other day. At four million years, they are the youngest mountains in the world. Ongoing tectonic activity in India is forcing sections of the mountains up by almost an inch per year. It is mid July as we make our way south towards the Himalayan range. I can feel myself in the heart of Tibet here at this altitude. I can also see the mountains bearing the marks of continental drift and I try to conjure up images of the cosmic collision.

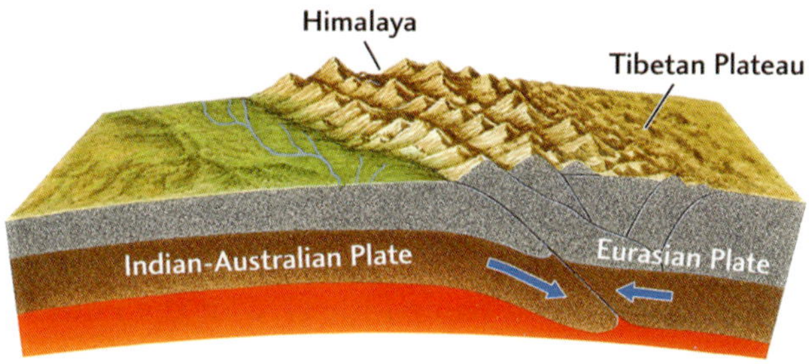

The creation of the Himalayas

Living with the same set of people for two months in such close proximity, I begin feeling like I am one of a large family on the move. Everything that can happen on such a long trip – new connections, love affairs, arguments, fall outs – has happened. The breaks in our journey have particular significance for each member. This provides us with the time to do something we like best, whether it be soaking in the sun or rolling a smoke. My favourite pair are our two geologists, Professor Thakur and Professor Zen. They wait for the halts to take out their pick-axes and chip away at any rock surface in the vicinity.

From left to right: Zen and Thakur studying rocks; Tibetan reaction to our caravan is one of wonder and bemusement alike

A view of Mount Everest

The film crew heads off to the Lakpa La Pass leaving the other members behind. This spot is famous because it offers a panoramic view of the Himalayas. If we are lucky we may even get a good view of the Everest. However, Hari has warned us to keep our expectations in check. He said Reinhold Messner, who climbed Mt Everest without oxygen cylinders, spent one whole month at the first base camp without seeing the summit because of the cloud cover. We have better luck. Our first glimpse of the world's highest peak occurs at 17,000 ft. Like Hari had told us, the sighting of the peak was momentary. It peeped out for a moment from behind the clouds and then disappeared again before the rest of the jeeps could arrive.

We stop at Shegar for the night. Also known as New Tingri, it is a village lying in the shadow of a huge fortress gone to ruins. The foundation of the once great fortress is perched regally on the cliff top. I send letters to my wife and children from the post office here – the highest in the world.

People in this secluded area of Tibet are born into a life of hardship, with the land buried in snow most of the time. Summertime here is a festival. The simple pleasures of life are enjoyed and celebrated to the fullest and we become part of the recreation wherever we go with our caravan and jeeps.

The village of Old Tingri lies in a grassland nurtured by the snow waters of the mountains. This village supplies the Sherpas, the native mountain people who have traditionally served as guides and porters to the Everest mountaineers. As elsewhere in Tibet, here too children magically appear and greet us as soon as we halt for some rest. Children in this country are considered special since any one of them may be an old and

The highest post office in the world

pious Lama reincarnated. After the Dalai Lama's death, a search commences for his new reincarnation. The chosen one must pass the test by displaying certain physical traits and mystical qualities which will single him out. Among other attributes, he must be able to know by sight the belongings of his previous incarnation.

It has been observed that reincarnated Lamas are invariably found in humble surroundings rather than affluent ones. The sceptics may point out that this is a deliberate ploy to ensure that one family doesn't claim hereditary rights to the title. I for one choose to believe otherwise … the humble in every tradition, the ones most open to the truth.

We have lunch at the ambitiously titled Everest View Hotel. It is a small inn serving noodles and buttered tea out of a quaint Tibetan kitchen. Wangdu is the only member of our expedition well versed in Tibetan. He engages a young Sherpa in conversation who refers to Mt Everest as Chomolungma, the Mother Goddess of the World.

New Tingri

Old Tingri

Old Tingri

'What does Chomolungma stand for? While for outsiders it is nothing more than a mountain peak that must be conquered, for Tibetans she is the Mother of the World. The Chomolungma's pristine whiteness is a symbol of purity of the enlightened heart and mind. Rangborang is a valley lying at the foot of Chomolungma. Once it was the natural habitat of wild animals such as the snow leopard, snow lion, old sheep, antelopes and wild ass. The vegetation was rich and varied. Once coral could be extracted here. The diverse variety of flowers attract birds of many kinds. The high altitude and resultant solitude have led to monks and ascetics retreating into the caves here for meditation. The Himalayas are like a sanctuary. The birds here are like the monks and the flowers are like the tinkling prayer bells and symbols of the chanting hall.'

The high passes of Tibet are adorned with prayer flags at all times. They remind me of open-air cathedrals where the worshippers congregate to admire and honour the natural wonders around them. Truck drivers upon reaching the top of a pass, halt and offer a ritual of thanks. Standing beside the fluttering flags, they take a few sacred verses and release them into the wind. I watch the blessings scatter to the four corners of the earth. I suddenly feel very close to the mountains here. Close enough to reach out and touch them.

Reaching the top of the Rongbuk river, we find Mt Everest covering the entire horizon. Initially known as Peak 15, its incredible height of 5 1/2 miles above sea level was first calculated by the Survey of India in 1852, using measurements taken from the Indian plains. According to legend, the then surveyor-director Radhanath Sikdar rushed into the Surveyor-General's office exclaiming, 'Sir, I have discovered the highest mountain in the world.' Peak 15 was subsequently renamed after Surveyor General of India, Sir George Everest.

Rongbuk monastery is perched on the edge of a desolate cliff with a panoramic view of the mountain. At 16,500 ft it has the distinction of being the highest spiritual retreat in the world. This is where we halt for the night. The Cultural Revolution razed the monastery to ruins and in the years following it served as a large rubbish heap for passing mountain climbers. Now we see a new stupa here. A number of buildings have been restored to offer basic facilities like tea and shelter for weary travellers like ourselves.

The initial Everest expeditions took off from Rongbuk after completing a month-long trek from Sikkim. Francis Younghusband in his new role as president of the Royal Geographical Society made the arrangements. By the 1920s the summit of Mt Everest had eclipsed Lhasa as the holy grail of the romantic traveller. Younghusband started believing that

The author filming the Everest in the backdrop of Rongbuk monastery

George Malory

scaling the peak tantamounted to a spiritual pilgrimage. The Tibetans disagreed. For them the Chomolungma was a holy site and intruding on its mountain spirits was a dangerous blasphemy. The monks attempted to dissuade and turn away the first climbers in vain.

The 1922 expedition included George Malory, easily the best climber of his day. Three separate attempts were made but the mission had to be called off when an avalanche wiped out seven Sherpas. The Rongbuk Lama arranged elaborate religious ceremonies for the dead Sherpas. Part of the rituals were concerned with the bad karma they had earned by attempting to scale the mountain.

Group photograph of the members of the 1924 Everest Expedition.
Standing from L to R: Irvine, Malory, Norton, Odell, Macdonald; Front row: Shebbeare, Bruce, Somervell, Beetham

In 1924, a second expedition was launched. The members set off in the snow carrying champagne, tins of quail in aspic, steel bottles of oxygen and leather waistcoats. John Noël was filming Malory and his young companion Andrew Irvine from below as they inched closer to the summit. Noël suddenly lost sight of them near the top. The rest of the party were forced to retreat because of blinding blizzards. But Malory and Irvin were never seen again.

Edmund Hillary and Tenzing Norgay after conquering the summit

Some like Younghusband believed that they died on the return journey after reaching the top. Others like the Rongbuk Lama was convinced that the Mother Goddess had demanded two more human sacrifices. One will never know what went wrong. But Malory and Irvin had shown to the world that the peak could indeed be conquered. Eight more expeditions from the north phase were thwarted by storms, avalanches and sheer altitude before the beginning of World War II.

On 29 May 1953, the New Zealander Edmund Hillary and his Sherpa Tenzing Norgay finally climbed to the top of the world from Nepal. The Swiss, the Chinese and

The Rongbuk monastery

The author and his companions beside Rongbuk river

The north face of Mount Everest

The highest summit of the world in its full glory

the Americans followed suit. In 1965 nine Indians, including Hari and Rawat, scaled the summit.

Rawat recollects – 'There were three of us on the same rope. Fu Dorzi lies buried under the snow somewhere up there and Hari who shortly became disabled forever. At the fourth base camp I shared my flask of tea with Hari. He said he'd never had better tea in his life. An avalanche struck our camp and swept away our stock of oxygen supply. We were at our wits' end. Come next morning, Fu Dorzi, Hari and I toiled away digging about in the snow until we found the oxygen cylinders again. It was nothing short of a miracle. We were young and nothing seemed impossible.'

The doctrine of Buddha spreads from Tibet, the northen land of the world; the summit of sky touching snow, his matchless insight without equal. The sun and the moon turning round its peak, a meditation radiating wisdom and compassion. Milarepa, Tibet's celebrated nature poet and most beloved saint, hails from this valley. Coming down from the Himalayas we pass through his valley en route to Nepal. It is said that he achieved perfect enlightenment here. Since the eleventh century he has been an inspiration for subsequent generations of Lamas till the present time. His songs of illumination are very popular. Legend has it that when his disciple Gampopa asked for his last instructions, Milarepa replied, 'What is needed is more effort, not more teachings.' Then he bared his calloused buttocks hardened by long years of meditation on a bare rock. 'That's my last instruction, son,' he said, 'do it.'

Milarepa as depicted in Tibetan art

We finally reach Nepal on 20 July. After the dry arid expanses of Tibet, it is a veritable explosion of greenery. The summer monsoon is here, ushering heavy rains on the Nepalese side of the Himalayas. A fragment of verse comes to mind. 'Cursorily we pass through all this world, otherwise, each place is a world of its own.' I bid Tibet and our journey farewell. A few last words rightly belong to

Hari who inspired and organized our expedition. They are from the concluding passages of his autobiography *Higher than Everest* (1997).

To the question, 'Why climb a mountain,' the famous mountaineer Malory is supposed to have answered, 'because it is there.' A good answer, but I wonder if it is quite complete. The experience is not only physical – it is also intensely emotional and even spiritual. The physical act of climbing a mountain has a kinship with the ascent of that inward spiritual mountain which every one has to climb sometime or the other. But whether the mountain you climb is physical or spiritual, the climb will change you. It will teach you much about you and the world.

EXPEDITION TEAM

Major H.P.S. Ahluwalia
Bholi Ahluwalia
Arun Bedi
Akhil Bakshi
Dr Rajesh Dogra
Dr Vikram Thakur
Dr K. Warikoo
Babar Hamid
Wangdus Kahlon
Gavin Hurtis
Hormozd Sorabjee
Navaz Bhatena
Nita Thapar
Falguni Matilal
Nazir Chagla
Harish Rawat

Italian Team

Umberto Scapagnini
Giovanni Scapagnini
Sergio Scapagnini
Paolo Sorbini

Film Crew

Goutam Ghose
Michael Haggiag
Jagganath Guha
Kabir Khan
Bejoy Anand

Impromptu celebration by opening a bottle of champagne upon completing 10,000 kms of the expedition

REFERENCES

Ahluwalia, H.P.S. 1997. *Higher than Everest*. Rupa & Co.

David-Néel, Alexandra. 1971. *Magic and Mystery in Tibet*. Dover Publications.

Hedin, Sven. 1903. *Central Asia and Tibet: Towards the Holy City of Lhasa*. London: Greenwood Press.

____. 1995. *Through Asia* Vols 1 & 2. India: Book Faith India.

Hopkirk, Peter. 1980. *Foreign Devils on the Silk Road: The Search for Lost Cities and Treasures of Chinese Central Asia*. London: John Murray.

____. 2006. *Trespassers on the Roof of the World: The Race for Lhasa*. London: John Murray.

Hunt, John. 1993. *The Ascent of Everest*. Hodder & Stoughton.

McCartney, Lady. 1986. *An English Lady in Chinese Turkestan*. Oxford University Press.

Stein, Aurel. 1998. *On Ancient Central Asian Tracks*. Delhi: Book Faith India.

Von Le Coq, Albert. 1928. *Buried Treasures of Chinese Turkestan: An Account of the Activities and Adventures of the Second and Third German Turfan Expeditions*. London: George Allen & Unwin.

Walker, Annabel. 1995. *Aurel Stein: Pioneer of the Silk Road*. London: John Murray.

Yule, Henry. 1903. *The Book of Ser Marco Polo the Venetian, Concerning the Kingdoms and Marvels of the East*. London: John Murray.

ACKNOWLEDGEMENTS

I am thankful to my friend Sergio Scapagnini who was instrumental for the connection with Major H.P.S. Ahluwalia, the leader of our Central Asian expedition.

Sagar Dutta, Ranjan Ghose and Debashish Mukherjee helped me restore the worn-out slides to quite a certain degree of satisfaction. We have also used some additional photographs taken by the second unit cinematographer Kabir Khan and my assistant Bejoy Anand. I am grateful to them.

I fondly remember the contribution of my poet friend Ain Rasheed Khan in writing the original script of the film. I am thankful to Sulagna Mukhopadhyay and Raja Mukhopadhyay for the transcription and my dear friend S.V. (Raju) Raman for revision of the text of the original soundtrack. Eminent writer Kunal Basu was kind enough to write the foreword with much love and compassion.

Last but not the least – Bikash Niyogi and the team at Niyogi Books who pursued me for long enough to publish this. The editor Sucharita Ghosh deserves full appreciation for her meticulous work and Pinaki De has designed the book with a rare passion. A big thank you to my wife Neelanjana Ghose without whose constant coordination and support, this would not have been possible.

INDEX

Note: Page numbers followed by "*f*" indicate figures.

T

U

W

X

Y

Z

ROUTE FOLLOWED BY THE AUTHOR AND HIS TEAM

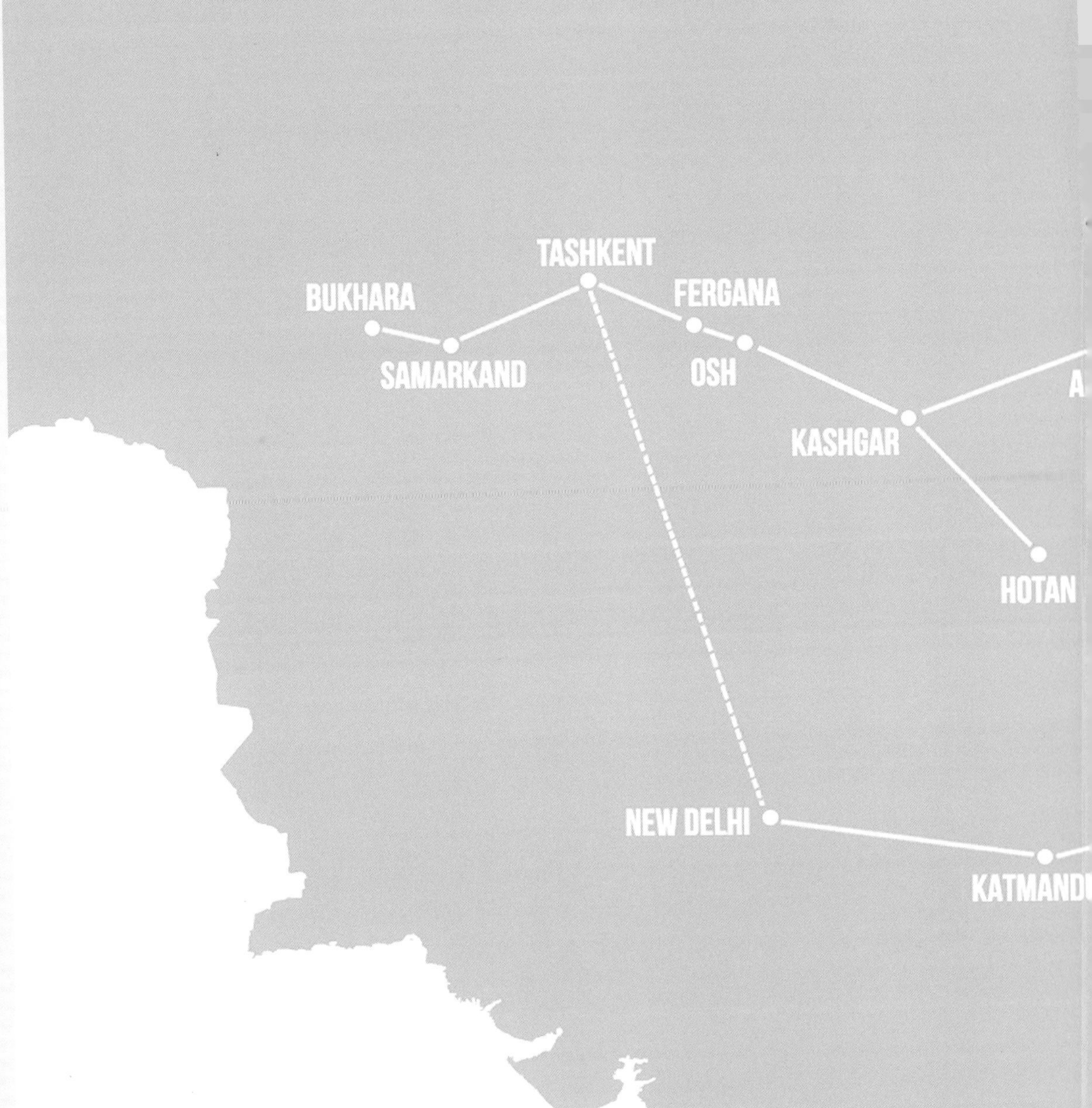